Strategic Marketing Planning and Evaluation

24

Marketing in Action Series
Series Editor: Norman Hart

Lively and 'easy to read', each book in the 'Marketing in Action' series is a clear, concise, action-oriented and up-to-date summary of a specific marketing topic. The books avoid jargon and provide busy marketers with valuable, practical step-by-step guidance. Ideal for marketers in organisations of any size, the books will also appeal to students studying for formal qualifications in marketing (CIM, CAM).

In producing this series, the advice and assistance has been sought of a prestigious editorial panel representing the principal professional bodies, trade associations and business schools.

The Series Editor for the Marketing in Action books is Norman Hart who is a writer of some ten books himself. He currently runs his own marketing consultancy, and is also an international lecturer on marketing, public relations and advertising at conferences and seminars.

Already available in the series:

A Practical Guide to Integrated Marketing Communications
Tom Brannan
How to Produce Successful Advertising
David Farbey
Successful Product Management
Stephen Morse
Getting the Best from Agencies
Geoffrey Smith
The Effective Use of Sponsorship
David Wragg
Creating Effective Marketing Communications
Daniel Yadin
Relationship Marketing
Merlin Stone and Neil Woodcock

Forthcoming titles in the series are:

Branding
Geoff Randall
Introduction to Marketing
Geoff Lancaster and Paul Reynolds
Direct Marketing
Margaret Allen
Marketing a Service
Ian Ruskin-Brown
Sales and Sales Management
Chris Horsman
International Marketing
Keith Lewis and Matthew Housden

Available from all good bookshops, or to obtain further information please contact the publishers at the address below:

Kogan Page Ltd
120 Pentonville Road
London N1 9JN
Tel: 0171 278 0433
Fax: 0171 837 6348

Strategic Marketing Planning and Evaluation

Geoffrey Lancaster and Lester Massingham

Series Editor: Norman Hart

KOGAN PAGE

YOURS TO HAVE AND TO HOLD

BUT NOT TO COPY

First published in 1996

Kogan Page Limited
120 Pentonville Road
London N1 9JN

© Geoff Lancaster and Lester Massingham, 1996

British Library Cataloguing in Publication Data

A CIP record for this book is available from the British Library.

ISBN 0 7494 1784 6

Typeset by DP Photosetting, Aylesbury, Bucks
Printed and bound in Great Britain by Biddles Ltd, Guildford and King's Lynn

Contents

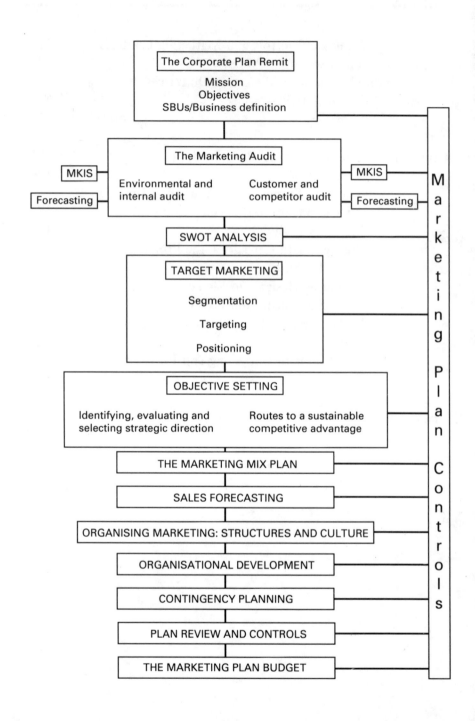

The Corporate Plan Remit

Mission
Objectives
SBUs/Business definition

The Marketing Audit

MKIS

Forecasting

Environmental and
internal audit

Customer and
competitor audit

MKIS

Forecasting

SWOT ANALYSIS

TARGET MARKETING

Segmentation

Targeting

Positioning

OBJECTIVE SETTING

Identifying, evaluating and
selecting strategic direction

Routes to a sustainable
competitive advantage

THE MARKETING MIX PLAN

SALES FORECASTING

ORGANISING MARKETING: STRUCTURES AND CULTURE

ORGANISATIONAL DEVELOPMENT

CONTINGENCY PLANNING

PLAN REVIEW AND CONTROLS

THE MARKETING PLAN BUDGET

Marketing Plan Controls

Chapter 1
Strategic Marketing Planning

INTRODUCTION

Many managers are now familiar with the tools and concepts of modern marketing. Marketing has evolved in most organisations from being viewed essentially as an adjunct of sales to a fully fledged separate functional area of business which is central to long-run organisational success. No longer must the marketing function fight to establish itself as being vital to this success. Similarly, over the years, those responsible for marketing in companies have become more skilled and professional in their application and use of marketing techniques and concepts. At the most senior levels of organisations the notion of the marketing concept and the need to be marketing oriented are now well understood. However, as perhaps one would expect from a functional area charged with meeting the constantly changing needs of the dynamic market, marketing itself, both in a conceptual and functional sense, is evolving and changing. Key among these changes to marketing concepts and practices has been the trend towards an ever more strategic perspective and approach to the planning and implementation of marketing in organisations. It is this strategic perspective and approach to marketing planning which forms the focus of this text.

It is assumed that the reader is familiar with the basic marketing concept and possibly some of the basic tools and techniques of marketing. What we have tried to do here, then, is to bring together contemporary thinking and developments in marketing which illustrate the need for, and the approaches to, a systematic process of strategic marketing planning. In order to do this we have developed a logical framework for developing and implementing the strategic marketing plan. This framework, which is outlined in this chapter, forms the basis for the remaining chapters in the book and is shown in Figure 1.1 on page 17. We will outline and discuss this framework shortly, but it is important to stress that this framework has been developed over several years and is tried and tested in both the teaching of strategic marketing to post-graduate students and prac- tising marketing managers, and in consultancy activities concerned with developing strategic marketing plans across a wide range of industries and organisations. Having stressed this, however, this text is aimed primarily at the practising marketing manager who is charged with the responsibility of developing strategic marketing plans for the organisation. The emphasis is very much on developing practical tools and concepts which can be applied by any manager who has been charged with this responsibility.

Before we examine and discuss our strategic marketing planning framework in this chapter, it would be useful first to explore the nature and development of a strategic approach to marketing planning.

BACKGROUND AND DEVELOPMENT

There is often considerable confusion regarding the nature of strategic marketing planning, including, for example, aspects such as the distinction between 'strategic' and 'tactical' plans, the difference between the 'strategic planning process', and the 'strategies' them- selves, and so on. In addition, it is often not clear why marketing planning needs increasingly to be strategic in nature. We shall deal with some of these issues here.

A Working Definition

There are probably as many definitions and certainly descriptions of strategic marketing as there are text books in this area. Sometimes these different definitions give a different flavour regarding the nature and meaning of strategic marketing, depending upon the perspectives and experiences of the particular author. For example, some definitions stress that strategic marketing should achieve a 'viable fit' between the organisation and its environment (sometimes termed 'strategic fit'). Others put more emphasis on strategic marketing as a process of seeking and maintaining a 'differential advantage'. Yet others stress the notion that strategic marketing centres on 'product-market investment decisions' which encompass the product-market scope of the business.

Doubtless, each of these different perspectives as to the nature of strategic marketing provide a potentially useful insight into the process of developing strategic marketing plans. However, for the student of strategic marketing and perhaps more so for the practitioner in this area, the lack of agreement as to the precise nature and scope of strategic marketing planning serves only to confuse. Nevertheless, we do need to have at least a working definition of strategic marketing which captures the essence of the process and which enables us to develop the systematic framework of strategic marketing planning which is so necessary to the development of effective plans. At the risk of adding to the confusion which stems from different definitions, therefore, the following is offered as our working definition of strategic marketing in the context of this text.

The essence of strategic marketing is the ability to make explicit marketing decisions within a dynamic market and organisational environment, through a systematic process to achieve position, survival, growth and sustained competitive advantage within specified time horizons and acknowledged resource constraints.

We shall examine the implications of this definition with regard to the specific steps and stages in strategic marketing planning later in this chapter and indeed throughout the rest of the text. But first it would be useful to trace briefly the development of a more strategic approach to marketing, together with some of the important characteristics of such an approach to the development of marketing plans.

Development of a Strategic Approach to Marketing

A number of factors have given rise to the need for a more strategic approach to strategic marketing. Some of the more important of these factors are as follows:

❑ The pace of change.
❑ Environmental interconnectedness and complexity.
❑ Technological innovation.
❑ Increased customer affluence and education.
❑ Increased competition.
❑ Globalisation.
❑ Increased organisational complexity and size.

These, then, are some of the more important factors that give rise to the need for a more strategic approach to marketing. Overall, these factors mean that it no longer makes commercial sense to rely upon 'gut feeling' and primitive planning tools. But what distinguishes a strategic from a non-strategic approach to marketing planning? The following are some of the key characteristics of a strategic perspective on marketing planning:

❑ A proactive approach: strategic marketing planning is based on attempting to influence and shape events, including demand rather than reacting to trends and changes as and when they occur.
❑ Longer planning horizons: a strategic approach to marketing planning encompasses longer time horizons for plans than a less strategic approach. Although planning horizons differ between companies and industries, a strategic marketing planning approach would normally encompass time horizons of anything between three and ten years.
❑ Customer-oriented planning: although long accepted as a key tenet of the marketing concept, strategic marketing planning must pay more than lip service to the need to be customer oriented. Everyone and everything in the organisation must be geared to identifying, participating and satisfying customer needs.
❑ Company considerations: strategic marketing planning must also be based on an in-depth and realistic appraisal of company

considerations so that strategic marketing plans reflect company aspirations, and corporate resources and constraints.

❏ Competitor considerations: a major facet of strategic marketing planning is the fact that competitor considerations are as important as customer and company elements. As we shall see in today's environment, companies need to be as much competitor as customer oriented.

❏ Information based: effective strategic marketing plans are based on accurate and timely information and the systems which provide it. Increasingly, information for strategic decision-making is 'on line' and designed to anticipate events.

Benefits of a Strategic Approach to Marketing Planning

Although we have outlined some of the factors that have given rise to the need for a strategic approach to marketing planning, understandably exhortations to adopt a more strategic approach are unlikely to be successful unless there are some clear benefits to adopting and implementing such an approach in an organisation. This is particularly true where, as is the case, this more strategic approach is inevitably more complex and difficult for the marketing planner. There are several benefits which accrue to the organisation and its planners from the adoption of a more strategic approach to marketing planning. These include:

❏ Increased motivation from both marketing and non-marketing staff associated with the planning process.

❏ Improved co-ordination between the different functional areas of the business with respect to competitive marketing strategies.

❏ Decreased uncertainty.

❏ Increased control over the company's future.

❏ Overall, an increased chance of achieving long-run organisational objectives together with all the advantages which attend and accrue from this.

THE STRATEGIC MARKETING PLANNING FRAMEWORK

As mentioned earlier, the major part of this text is built around a tried and tested framework for developing strategic marketing plans and we shall be using this framework throughout subsequent chapters. However, one of the major problems often encountered by those involved in strategic marketing planning is how to grasp the key elements of the process and, more often, how these elements are linked together in a systematic way. Again, we find that each text in this area will have its own suggested schema or framework. Our framework is shown in Figure 1.1 and you should now spend some time considering this framework before we proceed to outline the key elements shown in the framework in the remainder of the chapter.

We are not suggesting that this is the only way to order the strategic marketing planning process, but we would reiterate that it is a framework which we have found to be useful, logical and practical for this purpose. We shall now briefly outline each of the key elements in the framework before we discuss them in more detail in subsequent chapters. The relevant chapters on each key element are indicated below.

The Corporate Plan Remit

One of the most frequent confusions in planning management is the difference and relationships between corporate plans and planning, and strategic marketing plans and planning. At one extreme there is the view that corporate and marketing strategic plans are synonymous. Alternatively, there is the belief that the role of marketing in corporate planning is no different from that of other functional areas within a business.

We take the view that there is a key difference between marketing and corporate strategic plans, and that strategic marketing planning needs to be carried out in the context of the corporate strategic plan. Having said this, marketing lies at the heart of a company's planning process and has perhaps the leading role in helping both to shape and support corporate strategic planning. It is not possible, therefore, to plan a company's marketing activities in isolation from either

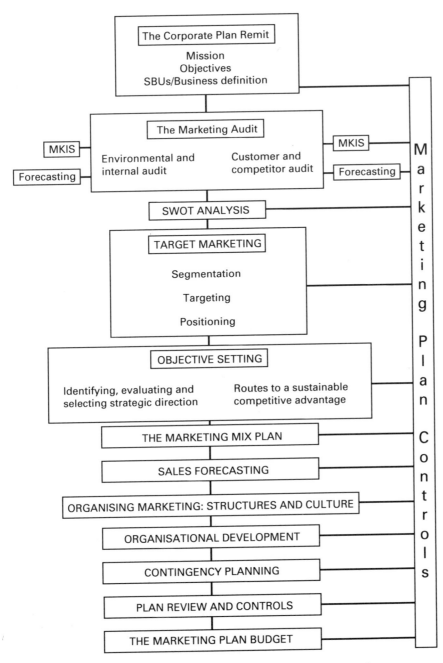

Figure 1.1   The strategic marketing plan: an overview

A company's marketing activities will function most effectively when they interact with the corporate planning process.

corporate strategies or other business functions. Consequently, the strategic marketing planning process must be firmly based in a total corporate planning system. This must be a two-way process with corporate plans both inputting to and effecting marketing strategies, and the marketing function, in particular through its analysis and forecasting activities, inputting to and effecting the corporate planning process itself.

Effectively, corporate plans and objectives should reflect the marketing functions analyses which encompass factors such as strengths and weaknesses, opportunities and threats (SWOT), competitor and customer analyses, and so on, each of which will be considered later and in more detail in subsequent chapters. In turn, however, the corporate plan which these analyses and inputs from marketing help to shape also serve to constrain and shape strategic marketing objectives and plans, including, for example, the choice of target markets, the marketing mix, marketing tactics, and so on.

Of particular relevance to strategic marketing planning activities are the areas of corporate mission statements and business definition, overall corporate objectives, and an analysis of organisational resources, particularly with regard to the identification of organisation constraints. These elements, together with the important related concept of Strategic Business Units, or SBUs as they are often referred to, are the subject of Chapter 2.

The Marketing Audit

All planning requires an analysis of the current situation ('where we are now') as a prelude to determining future objectives ('where we want to be') and strategies for achieving these ('how we are going to get there'). In marketing, the analysis of the current situation, including future trends and changes, is encompassed by the planning tool of the 'marketing audit'. The marketing audit is a systematic and wide-ranging analysis of the current situation, encompassing the broader marketing environment, competitor and customer analysis, and an assessment of the company's internal capacity. This analysis in turn forms the basis of the assessment of a company's strengths and weaknesses, and the opportunities and threats which it faces. The marketing audit will require the forecasting of future trends and developments, and must be linked to an effective marketing information system. The nature, purpose and approaches to conducting the marketing audit, together with a brief outline of some of the more important forecasting techniques associated with this stage of the marketing planning process, are the subject of Chapters 3 and 4. In Chapter 3 we consider the steps involved in conducting an audit of the external environment of the organisation and the internal marketing audit. In Chapter 4 we look at the analyses and audits of customers and competitors. In turn, these audits feed into and become the basis of the SWOT analysis which is discussed in Chapter 5. The marketing information system, because of its importance throughout the strategic marketing planning process, is considered in Chapter 11.

The SWOT Analysis

This element of the strategic marketing plan essentially represents the output of the marketing audit analysis, and in particular the analysis of the environmental factors and the internal appraisal part of the marketing audit. Many managers are now familiar with this well-known acronym which stands for strengths, weaknesses, opportunities and threats. A key part of the marketing planning process is the assessment of these SWOT factors, together with an evaluation of the implications for marketing objectives and plans. The SWOT analysis is the subject of Chapter 5.

SEGMENTATION, TARGETING AND POSITIONING

It is now widely accepted that the three interrelated aspects of segmenting, targeting and positioning in markets are among the most important steps in developing strategic marketing plans. It is important to remember that these three steps are really part of one overall process of matching distinctive competencies to the needs of specific customer groups in a market and ensuring that the product market offering of the organisation has a competitive position or edge against other companies. Segmentation is the first step in the process and consists of identifying groups of customers with similar needs and wants as potential, distinct and separate possible target markets. As we shall see, there are a number of ways to segment markets, both consumer and business-to-business, and a number of considerations in the evaluation and selection of appropriate bases for segmenting markets. Segmentation is covered in Chapter 6. Having identified potential market segments, the marketing planner must then select the most appropriate segments to target. This in turn entails matching distinctive competencies of the organisation to specific market segments where these competencies are likely to give the greatest competitive advantage. It also entails evaluation by the marketer of the relative market attractiveness of the different segments identified. Finally, the marketer must develop positioning strategies within the different targeted segments in order to achieve a predetermined position in the target segments vis-à-vis competition. Targeting, including the techniques of evaluating market attractiveness which are essential to the targeting process, is discussed in Chapter 7. The third and final step in this process, namely, positioning, which involves determining how a product or brand is intended to be perceived by the market and on what basis it will be differentiated against competition, is the subject of Chapter 8.

When groups of customers with similar needs and wants are identified as possible target markets, the appropriate segments can be targeted and the product positioned effectively against existing brands.

MARKETING STRATEGIES

Identifying, Evaluating and Selecting Strategic Direction

At this stage in the development of the strategic marketing plan we are able to move into the development of specific strategic marketing objectives and strategies. There are a number of aspects to this. First, we must decide the broad strategic direction which we are going to take. There are a number of frameworks for configuring the options with regard to these alternative strategic directions. The first of these frameworks, which is known as 'the product market scope matrix' is based on configuring these around different combinations of product market strategies. For example, objectives can relate to growth in existing product markets, new products for existing markets, new markets for existing products, or new markets and new products.

This taxonomy of possible broad strategic directions and objectives for marketing was developed by Igor Ansoff as long ago as the 1960s but is still widely accepted as a useful way of delineating the alternatives which are available to the marketer. A second framework for delineating strategic marketing options is based on the stage at which a product is at in its overall sales life-cycle. For perhaps obvious reasons, this framework has come to be known as the 'product life cycle' concept. Finally, a third framework for identifying alternative strategic objectives and directions is based on examining the current 'portfolio' of products or services in an organisation with a view to identifying what strategies are necessary to survive and grow in the future. There are many so-called portfolio models, but we shall examine one of the simplest and yet most robust of these, namely the Boston Consulting Group's (BCG) product market matrix. The notion of alternative objectives and directions for strategic growth, together with these three frameworks are discussed in Chapter 9.

Routes to a Sustainable Competitive Advantage

Having identified and selected from the alternative strategic objectives and directions, the second key element of developing marketing strategies is the selection between the strategic alternatives for achieving a sustainable competitive advantage. This step of the marketing planning process involves selecting how the company will compete for customers. As we shall see, there are a number of possible broad strategies which can be used as a basis for competitive advantage. These broad strategies are often referred to as 'generic strategies'. The importance and meaning of developing a sustainable competitive advantage, together with the broad alternative generic strategies for achieving this advantage are discussed in Chapter 10.

Developing the Marketing Mix

At this stage we can move to the development of more detailed marketing plans which encompass each of the elements of the marketing mix in an integrated and co-ordinated set of strategies and tactics designed to achieve the overall corporate and marketing objectives. These objectives were established earlier in the process and are based on implementing the selected marketing strategies in order to achieve a sustainable competitive advantage in the organisation's target markets. The marketing mix plan, including strategies both for the conventional 'four ps' of product, price, place and promotion, and possibly for the extended mix, including people, process and physical evidence, is determined by each and all of the previous stages in developing the strategic marketing plan. Planning the marketing mix is the subject of Chapter 12.

Sales Forecasting

Having developed plans for the marketing mix, we can move to the stage of sales forecasting which is particularly important for the development of the key performance indicators in the strategic marketing plan and the development of budgets. In addition, sales forecasting is a key input to the development of other plans in the organisation, such as production planning. These areas are covered in Chapter 13.

Organising for and Implementing Strategic Marketing Plans

Marketing plans can only be implemented when the necessary structures, systems and people are in place.

Plans are nothing unless they are turned into action. A key part of the strategic marketing planning process is to ensure that the necessary structures, systems and people are in place in order to implement the plan. In particular, it is important to ensure that the organisational structure and systems are sufficiently marketing oriented. The marketer must therefore ensure that the appropriate organisational structure is in place to implement the strategic marketing plan. This element is covered in Chapter 14, together with the steps which are required to build a marketing culture. Building a marketing culture and a strategic approach to marketing in the organisation may require in turn organisational development and change. This aspect is covered in Chapter 15.

Contingencies, Controls and Budgets

The final elements of the strategic marketing plan involve establishing and implementing a set of reviews and controls so that the plan is reviewed on a regular basis. Once again, this will require an effective marketing information system (MkIS) as discussed in Chapter 11. Any contingency plans highlighted from the earlier planning stages will also need to be developed and, of course, implemented where necessary. Finally, the plan should be costed and each area of marketing activity allocated budgets as part of the total budgetary control system of the organisation. Systems will need to be in place in order to control costs and, where appropriate, to assess the financial performance of the organisation. These areas of the strategic marketing plan form the focus of Chapters 16, 17 and 18.

Summary

In this chapter we have introduced the nature of strategic marketing planning. We have also traced briefly the reasons for the development of a more strategic approach to marketing. Essentially, however, we have sought to introduce you to a framework for developing and implementing strategic marketing plans around which the remainder of this text is based. The general shortened framework for such planning is sometimes referred to under the acronym 'MOST' which stands for: Mission; Objectives; Strategy; Tactics.

We are now ready to explore the key steps in this framework in more detail.

Chapter 2
The Corporate Plan Remit

INTRODUCTION

In this chapter we begin the process of examining the steps in the strategic marketing planning process by looking at the corporate context within which strategic marketing planning takes place. As already mentioned in Chapter 1, strategic marketing plans need to be consistent with, and supportive of, the overall corporate plans of the organisation. Indeed, it is from such overall corporate plans that marketing plans are as such derived in large measure. We have also seen that there is often confusion regarding the distinction and relationships between the corporate and strategic marketing plans. We have suggested that the two are different although very closely interrelated. The corporate plan sets objectives and strategies for the organisation as a whole and encompasses all functions in the organisation, whereas the strategic marketing plan is concerned only with strategies which pertain to markets and customers. We have also suggested, however, that a key input to the development of corporate plans is the analysis of markets, customers and competitors, and in particular the assessment of marketing opportunities and threats provided by the marketing function. Corporate plans are in large measure developed from the analysis provided by the marketing function. In turn, though, as already suggested, it is not possible or appropriate to develop marketing strategies without reference to the corporate plan remit. In effect, the corporate plan serves to delineate and shape the direction and nature of marketing strategies in the organisation, alongside strategies for each and every other functional area in the business. Of particular importance to the development of marketing and other strategies are the elements of corporate mission statements, corporate objectives, the concept of strategic business units (SBUs), and the related and extremely important process of business definition. We shall therefore explore the meaning and significance of these elements of the corporate planning process with regard to the development of strategic marketing plans.

THE CORPORATE PLANNING PROCESS

Strategy is a means by which an organisation achieves its objectives. However, there are various levels of strategic planning in an organisation. At the top of this hierarchy of planning levels is the overall corporate strategic plan. This plan sets the direction for the organisation as a whole and overall strategies which will be used to achieve predetermined corporate objectives which are also set during the corporate planning process. These corporate objectives and strategies should then filter down to subsequent levels in the hierarchy of planning so that functional strategies, including those for marketing, reflect and support the corporate strategies. Corporate strategies are concerned with the scope of an organisation's activities and have major resource implications for the organisation. They are planned at the very highest level and are long term in focus, often encompassing planning horizons of up to and beyond five years into the future. There are many elements to the corporate planning process, but in developing strategic marketing plans the marketing manager must understand and appreciate those elements of the corporate planning process which are particularly important to these marketing plans. We shall now consider the more important of these elements, explaining their significance and relevance to the marketing manager.

Understanding and appreciating the corporate planning process is very important when strategic marketing plans are being developed.

CORPORATE MISSION STATEMENTS

The corporate mission statement represents the framework for the culture and functioning of the entire business, ranging through the operation of each major functional area of the business through to the activities and approaches of each and every individual employed by the organisation. Needless to say, therefore, the corporate mission statement is fundamental to the formulation and selection of marketing objectives and strategies. Because of this, it is vital that marketing management are made aware of the corporate mission statement and understand its implications for the development of marketing strategies. In fact, as mentioned earlier, the corporate mission statement itself may in part be derived from analyses conducted by the marketing function.

In essence, the corporate mission statement defines the overall strategic thrust of an organisation and the underpinning unique characteristics which delineate the organisation. As we might expect, the nature and content of corporate mission statements vary between organisations and it is therefore difficult to be specific about what constitutes a 'typical' mission statement. It might be easier to understand the function of mission statements if we examine a hypothetical statement for an imaginary organisation as follows:

> As a company we intend to serve the interests of all major stakeholders in the organisation, including customers, shareholders, employees and the local community, to the best of our ability. We shall endeavour to be caring, ethical and professional in all our dealings with stakeholders and other interested parties in the conduct of our business and shall give due concern to the protection of the environment. The scope of our business will be concerned with the development of agricare products for international markets with specific reference to cereal crop farmers. The organisation will continue to be vertical in nature, encompassing the supply of raw materials, manufacture and distribution to customers. The emphasis will be on quality and value, with high levels of customer service, and utilising the most advanced technology of manufacture and distribution. Particular importance is attached to new product development and innovation based on company research and development in order to develop new products and new markets.

We can see that such statements are wide-ranging and encompass major policy areas of the business. In effect, the mission statement, as mentioned earlier, serves to capture and reflect the essential character of the business and how it will operate perhaps over a 10- to 20-year period. As such, the formulation of the corporate mission statement should be carried out by the most senior managers in the company and may require substantial time and investment in analyses as an input to the process. There is no doubt that formulating corporate mission statements is not easy and in some companies it may take several years to develop effective examples.

An effective mission statement should have the following general characteristics or qualities:

Considerable time and care should be invested in formulating the corporate mission statement which should capture the unique characteristics of a business and reflect its long-term future.

❑ *Be neither too specific nor too vague*: many mission statements are much too vague to be of use in directing the organisation for the future. On the other hand, the mission statement should not be too constraining so as to debar management effectively from pursuing future opportunities as the environment changes.
❑ *Be communicated*: it is pointless having mission statements if only the people at the top are aware of their content and implications. The mission statement must be communicated to and understood not only by all functions and employees in the organisation, but also by all other stakeholders and parties affected by the organisation.
❑ *Be motivating*: the mission statement should serve to motivate and encourage all those with a stake in the organisation.
❑ *Be customer oriented*: the mission statement should be outward looking and in particular should reflect an acknowledgement and acceptance of the need to focus on customers as a key to organisational success. However, this should be balanced by an awareness of the interests of other key stakeholders in the business.
❑ *Be realistic*: the mission statement needs to reflect what is possible rather than only desirable. This in turn means that the mission statement must reflect considerations regarding, for example, the resources and skills of the organisation, and the requirements and constraints of the environment in which it operates.

Returning to our hypothetical mission statement, we can also see some of the key functions of the mission statement, particularly with respect to the development of strategic marketing plans. The mission statement should help to delineate and define the following:

❑ The overall purpose of the organisation.

❑ The industry scope – that is, the major markets in which the company will operate.

❑ Customer segments – that is, the major customer groups within these markets which the company will serve.

❑ The geographical scope.

❑ The main competitive thrust – that is, the key factors which will serve as the bases for competition.

❑ The range of business operations – for example, the extent of vertical integration in the organisation and the extent to which key functional areas such as research and development are to figure in the overall competitive profile of the company.

We can see from the list of ways in which the mission statement helps to delineate and define the character and functioning of the organisation, the significance and impact of the mission statement for the development of marketing objectives and strategies. Effectively, much of marketing strategy is in essence determined, or at least significantly shaped, by the overall mission statement. So, for example, many elements of the strategic marketing plan, such as target marketing, positioning, marketing objectives, core marketing strategies and the marketing mix itself, stem from and must reflect the overall corporate mission statement. These elements will be discussed in subsequent chapters.

Related to the corporate mission statement, and in some ways just as significant for the development of strategic marketing plans, is the element in corporate planning of corporate objectives. It is to this element that we shall now turn our attention.

CORPORATE OBJECTIVES

Just as the corporate mission statement serves to shape and constrain the elements of the strategic marketing plan, so too do corporate objectives. For example, if one of the corporate objectives is for growth with specific targets being set for the organisation, clearly marketing strategies must be aimed at helping to achieve this growth target. As with the corporate mission statement, in fact, the process is two–way in that corporate objectives themselves are likely, in part at least, to derive from a detailed analysis of the market.

Typically, companies have objectives in several areas, any one, or all of which will affect the selection of marketing objectives and strategies. It is important to remember that in this context corporate objectives are likely to encompass more than simply financial objectives. In addition, corporate objectives may involve both qualitative and quantitative objectives. Below are listed examples of common areas for objectives in the contemporary organisation. We have divided these into qualitative and quantitative objectives.

Qualitative objectives	Quantitative objectives
Market standing/reputation	Profitability through, for example, return on capital employed (ROCE), return on investment (ROI)
Innovation	Liquidity
Management performance	Productivity
Public responsibility	Sales/market share
Organisational development	

As with all objectives, corporate objectives should possess a number of characteristics if they are to fulfil their roles of guiding action and serving as a basis for measurement and control. Ideally the objectives should be:

❑ *Realistic*: it is pointless setting objectives which are not achievable. On the other hand, of course, the objectives should serve to motivate individuals and functions to higher levels of performance over time.
❑ *Specific*: even with qualitative objectives, it is important to be as specific as possible regarding the outcomes encompassed by the objectives. Ideally, the objectives should also be measurable in order to serve better as a basis for control purposes. This is not always easy with some of the qualitative objectives.
❑ *Consistent*: where there are several corporate objectives, it is important that these are not inconsistent or incompatible. So, for

example, objectives for profit, say, should not make it impossible or even difficult to achieve objectives with respect to, say, social responsibility. Another aspect of consistency is the importance of ensuring that objectives at different levels in the planning hierarchy, including marketing objectives, are also consistent, one with another.

❏ *Communicated*: it is vital that objectives are communicated and wherever possible agreed with those who are charged with the responsibility of achieving them. For this reason objective setting is best conducted as a two-way process rather than the objectives being specified simply as an edict from above.

It is not too difficult to see, therefore, the importance and relevance of corporate objectives to the development of strategic marketing plans. Some writers use the acronym 'SMART' when looking at objectives. This stands for: Specific; Measurable; Attainable; Realistic and Time based. We can now move to the third element in our corporate planning process, namely, decisions which relate to the configuration of the organisation into individual strategic business units.

DELINEATING STRATEGIC BUSINESS UNITS (SBUs)

In most organisations of any size the organisation serves a variety of markets, with several different products aimed at different customer groups. Depending on the organisation, there may be different degrees of congruency between different areas of the business. For example, in the conglomerate organisation, the organisation may serve markets as diverse as the supply of components for the aerospace industry to the production and marketing of plastic buckets. In most contemporary business organisations, therefore, a decision has to be made as to how the business can be organised into coherent and viable individual units so that each unit can be managed and controlled effectively on an individual basis, while at the same time at the corporate level the different parts of the business can be managed effectively on a collective basis. There are several possible organisational approaches to managing the problems of complexity and diversity in the modern business organisation, but one of the most successful and therefore popular approaches in recent years has been to organise the business into strategic business units (or as they are usually referred to, SBUs). This requires that, at the corporate level, decisions must be made as to the appropriate bases for splitting the business in organisational terms into individual SBUs.

Delineating separate SBUs in an organisation is by no means an easy task. However, ideally an SBU has the following characteristics which serve as a guide to the corporate planner as to how to delineate SBUs in the business:

❑ An SBU should have its own customers and competitors.
❑ An SBU, in concept, should be able to be operated as a separate business.
❑ An SBU should be able to identify and isolate its own individual costs and revenues and should be largely responsible for its own profits and losses.
❑ An SBU should have its own management team which is responsible for the operation of the unit.

These characteristics can be used to delineate individual strategic business units in the organisation. So far as the development of strategic marketing plans is concerned, the application of the concept of SBUs in a business has several important implications, two of which are most important. First, it allows decisions to be made regarding the relative *balance* between the different SBUs in the business and in particular, reflecting this, decisions as to resource allocations to different parts of the business. Secondly, organising the business into strategic business units allows the development of meaningful business definitions and strategic marketing plans for each individual SBU in the business. These two implications of the application of the SBU concept in corporate planning are outlined in more detail below.

Organising a company into strategic business units enables it to reach the right decisions on the allocation of resources and to develop meaningful business definitions and marketing plans.

BALANCING SBUs/RESOURCE ALLOCATION

In the multi-market business with several SBUs, the corporate planner must decide what the balance between these different SBUs is to be in the business, with the required balance, once decided, being achieved through decisions regarding resource allocation to the different SBUs. For example, the corporate planner needs to balance parts of the business which are growing and are perhaps therefore heavy users of cash against parts of the business which are more mature and, therefore, although not growing, may generate large amounts of positive net cash flow. Similarly, the corporate planner must achieve a balance between yesterday's products and tomorrow's breadwinners. As a result, the corporate planner must decide which parts of the business to invest in heavily and to allow to grow, which parts of the business to maintain with moderate levels of investment, and which parts of the business to withdraw investment from and effectively harvest or divest.

Clearly, as a result of these decisions different SBUs will be required to perform differently and also will have different levels of investment. Needless to say, strategic marketing plans in the SBU which is receiving substantial investment in order to grow, are likely to be very different from those plans which are appropriate to the SBU which is being harvested or which is a candidate for divestment.

BUSINESS DEFINITION/STRATEGIC MARKETING PLANNING AT THE SBU LEVEL

As most marketers are now aware, a key concept in the development of marketing plans is the notion of business definition. In the past, the process of business definition has often proved problematical in the multi-product market business. This has been due partly to mis-understandings regarding the nature and purpose of business definition and partly because of the difficulties of defining the business in a diversified organisation. The concept of strategic business units enables much more effective business definitions and, in fact, each strategic business unit should have its own business definition. These business definitions should specify the following elements:

❏ The customer groups to be served by the strategic business unit.
❏ The functions or needs of the customers which the SBU provides.

❏ The technology utilised in the product or service solutions of the SBU.

For example, a business definition for a strategic business unit might be along the lines of, say:

> We are in the business of solving the liquid cooling and heating problems (customer needs) in the brewing industry (customer groups), utilising heat exchangers (technology).

It should be easy to see the significance and usefulness of such business definitions in the context of the development of strategic marketing plans. Without the organisation of the business into separate strategic business units, it is virtually impossible to develop meaningful business definitions and equally it is virtually impossible to develop meaningful and effective strategic marketing plans. In fact, it is extremely important to stress that the development of strategic marketing plans is at the level of each strategic business unit. In other words, each strategic business unit in an organisation should have its own separate strategic marketing plan. The unit of analysis, therefore, for the development of strategic marketing plans outlined in this text is the individual strategic business unit. It is vital to remember this in considering the overview of strategic marketing planning which was developed in Chapter 1 and in understanding the stages shown in this process in the chapters which follow.

Summary

In this chapter we have considered the corporate planning framework within which strategic marketing plans are developed. Strategic marketing plans form but a subset of the overall corporate plan in an organisation, albeit in some ways perhaps the most important subset. Strategic marketing plans are constrained and shaped by overall corporate plans, and therefore the marketing planner needs to understand the nature of these constraints and shaping processes and how they relate to his or her own organisation. Of particular importance in affecting strategic marketing plans are the corporate planning elements of corporate mission statements, corporate objectives, delineation of strategic business units, and the related areas of resource allocation to SBUs and a business definition for each SBU.

Chapter 3
The Marketing Audit (1)

INTRODUCTION

The marketing audit is a key step in developing strategic marketing plans and involves assessing the company's present position, and the forces and factors both internal and external to the organisation which will affect it in the future. Because of this, the marketing audit needs to be a wide-ranging and in-depth analysis of many factors. The precise nature of the audit and its scope will vary from company to company but generally the audit will involve an analysis of *external* factors – that is, those factors outside the organisation, including, for example, the broader environmental factors, such as the political, economic, social–cultural, technological (PEST) and natural factors, and the more immediate environmental factors of customers and competitors. The audit will also encompass an analysis of *internal* factors encompassing the resources and skills of the organisation, including any deficiencies or weaknesses. Because of the importance of the marketing audit in developing strategic marketing plans and because of the scope and complexity involved, two chapters are devoted to this important area. In this chapter we shall consider the audit of the broader environmental factors, and the internal part of the audit. In the next chapter we shall consider those parts of the audit which encompass customer and competitor analyses. It is important, however, that these are seen as part of one process of conducting the marketing audit. In addition, the marketing audit itself feeds into the next stage of strategic marketing planning – namely the identification and evaluation of the key strengths and weaknesses, and the opportunities and threats facing the organisation. This so-called SWOT analysis is the subject of Chapter 5. All three chapters, then, essentially collectively form the audit and analysis part of the development of strategic marketing plans.

ENVIRONMENTAL ANALYSIS

The first element of the marketing audit is to analyse the key environmental forces and factors, together with any trends and changes in these factors, which will affect any future marketing objectives and plans. Trends and changes in the environment give rise to some of the most significant marketing opportunities and threats facing any organisation, and therefore need to be taken account of in developing future marketing plans. This process of analysing the environment, in the context of the marketing audit stage of planning, involves the following three steps:

1. Identifying the key environmental forces relevant to the development of future strategic marketing plans.
2. Forecasting future trends and changes in these factors.
3. Assessing the potential impact of these trends and changes in the organisation.

In this chapter we shall confine ourselves to discussing the issues in and approaches to the first two of these elements – namely, the identification and forecasting steps. Ultimately, of course, strategic marketing objectives and plans will need to be based on the third of these steps – namely, an assessment of the potential impact of forecast changes and trends in the key environmental forces which have been identified. The link to moving from the identification and forecasting steps of environmental analysis to the step of assessing the impact of these and their implications for marketing planning is provided by the opportunities and threats element of the overall SWOT analysis. We shall therefore discuss the third step of assessing the potential impact of trends and changes when we discuss the SWOT analysis in Chapter 5. We shall now turn our attention to the identification and forecasting of environmental forces.

Identifying key environmental forces

By definition, 'the environment' encompasses all those forces and factors outside the organisation. A problem in conducting the environmental analysis part of the marketing audit, therefore, is identifying the *key* factors which are pertinent to a particular organisation or, where appropriate, a particular strategic business unit.

In broad terms, we may identify distinct groups of environmental factors which, to a greater or lesser degree, potentially affect all industries and organisations. Conventionally, these groups are:

- ❑ Political factors (including legal and regulatory factors).
- ❑ Economic forces and factors.
- ❑ Socio-cultural forces and factors.
- ❑ Technological forces and factors.

These four groups of factors are so ubiquitous in strategic planning circles that they are often referred to as PEST (or STEP) factors.

In recent years, however, a fifth group of broad environmental factors has become important enough for strategic marketing planners to consider separately. This filth environmental factor is often referred to as the natural environmental. This category of environmental factors encompasses issues concerned with, for example, the depletion of natural resources, pollution from industry and products, and so on. These so-called 'green' issues have become sufficiently important to marketers for them to merit special consideration by many companies. Some writers now refer to the acronym 'PESTLE' where the final two letters stand for: Legal and Environmental.

Of course, while these broad categories of environmental factors may affect all companies over time, each category contains a myriad of forces and factors which affect different companies in different ways. For example, we can distinguish some of the following elements within each broad category:

Political/regulatory factors

- Privatisation versus nationalisation policies.
- International relationships.
- Regulations concerning trading practices.

- Regulations concerning monopolies and mergers.
- Public spending.
- Advertising and other promotional regulations.

Economic factors

- Economic growth.
- Income levels.
- Interest rates.
- Exchange rates.
- Balance of payment levels.
- Employment.
- Credit policies.
- Income distribution.
- Savings and debt.
- Taxation.

Socio-cultural factors

- The changing age structure of the population.
- Trends in family size.
- Changes in the amount and nature of leisure time.
- Changes in attitude towards health and lifestyles.
- Improved education.
- Changes in attitudes towards family roles.
- Changing work patterns.
- Equal opportunities.

Technological factors

- Automation.
- New methods of travel.
- New materials.
- Improved circulation.
- More powerful computing.

Natural factors

- Natural resource depletion.
- Pollution.
- Biodegradable materials.
- Changes in climate.

Clearly, it is neither possible nor useful to list each and every possible environmental element which might potentially need to be considered by the strategic marketing planner in this part of the marketing audit. As mentioned earlier, the key factors which the planner will need to consider, forecast and appraise will vary between each strategic business unit. Once again we see the significance of focusing the strategic marketing planning process around each individual strategic business unit. In developing strategic marketing plans for each SBU, the company must determine the *key* environmental forces and factors which need to be assessed. Thankfully, very often the most significant environmental forces and factors for each SBU will be relatively obvious. For example, a strategic business unit concerned with the marketing of alcoholic beverages will need to monitor carefully and to assess trends and changes in, say, the social factors affecting the consumption of alcohol, the legislation affecting the licensed trade, and any changes in taxation and particularly excise duties. Similarly, a company manufacturing microwave products would need to monitor and assess trends and changes in, say, eating habits, leisure time, working patterns, and gender issues.

The danger in suggesting that the identification of the most relevant environmental forces and factors is merely a matter of 'common sense' is that often what prove to be the most important environmental forces and factors to a company are not immediately obvious. For example, in the 1960s and 1970s many marketers of mechanical cash registers did not foresee the significance of the technological trend towards electronic products. For this reason, many of these marketers found themselves threatened and in many cases out of business owing to the growth of electronic and eventually computer-based cash registers. Similarly, entirely new forces and factors in the environment can emerge, often very rapidly and without warning, making it difficult, if not impossible, to monitor and appraise them in advance. It is important, therefore, to keep a broad perspective on what might constitute significant environmental forces and factors. A useful device in helping to achieve this broad perspective regarding what might constitute key environmental forces and factors is the definition of the business referred to in Chapter 2 where we suggested that an effective definition of the business encompasses customer needs, customer groups and technologies. Defining the business in this way for each strategic business unit at least helps to identify significant environmental factors which will need to be included in the marketing audit.

Defining the business effectively helps to keep a broad perspective on significant environmental factors and forces which can affect future trends.

Ideally, the identification of the key environmental factors, which in turn will need to be forecast and assessed with regard to their potential implications for the strategic marketing plan, should be done on a regular basis and preferably involving an interfunctional team of managers from different parts of the organisation. We would stress, however, that a checklist of key environmental factors which are to be the focus of analysis and assessment must be drawn up for each strategic business unit for which a strategic marketing plan is being developed.

Forecasting future trends and changes in key environmental forces

Trends and changes in the elements of the environment are significant for developing future marketing strategies. We shall discuss this significance in more detail in Chapter 5. At this stage, it is sufficient to point out that it is the trends and changes in the categories of environmental factors already outlined in this chapter that give rise to some of the most significant marketing opportunities and threats. Given that we are developing marketing plans for the future, therefore, it is important to try to forecast both the magnitude and direction of trends and changes in those environmental factors which have been identified as most significant.

A number of forecasting techniques may be useful in this process. The following techniques may be particularly relevant.

❑ Trend extrapolation.
❑ Trend correlation.
❑ Scenario building.
❑ Morphological analysis.
❑ Econometric modelling.
❑ Cross impact analysis.
❑ Expert opinion.

Ideally, a combination of techniques should be used. In the larger organisation, environmental forecasting might be part of the marketing information system in the organisation. In addition, it is possible to purchase commercially available environmental forecasts, such as those provided by the Henley Forecasting Centre in the United Kingdom.

A decision will have to be made regarding the time-scale which such forecasts will encompass and these may vary not only between different companies, and certainly between different industries, but also between the different elements of the environment being forecast. In some cases, forecasts may encompass time horizons of, say, up to 18 months or two years hence, but in other cases may involve time horizons of ten or more years. Some experts in this area have suggested that as a rule-of-thumb, the time horizon for environmental forecasting should be approximately twice as long as the duration of the strategic marketing plan. For example, if the plan encompasses a time horizon of five years, an appropriate time horizon for forecasting would be ten years.

Ensure that adequate systems are in place and the right personnel are available to conduct and produce environmental forecasts.

It is important to ensure that there are adequate systems in place for conducting such forecasts and that clear responsibilities are allocated for producing the forecasts. According to the circumstances, the marketing manager and the marketing team will be responsible sometimes for the forecasts; in larger organisations, however, it may be possible and preferable to appoint forecasting experts who are responsible for the scanning and forecasting process. It is important to note that many organisations do not have formal systems for analysing and distributing key environmental information to strategic marketing planners. In addition, all too often marketing managers in particular are too 'tied up' with day-to-day activities to provide enough time and attention to think about the long-term future.

These, then, are the two key steps of conducting an audit of the broader environment factors which, as mentioned earlier, will feed into the opportunities and threats analysis later in the strategic marketing planning process. The input to the other half of our SWOT analysis is provided by that part of the marketing audit which covers an internal analysis of the strategic business unit, and it is to this analysis that we now turn our attention.

INTERNAL ANALYSIS

In this part of the chapter we shall look at that aspect of the marketing audit which is concerned with assessing the internal elements and operation of the strategic business unit. As with the analysis of the broad environmental factors discussed earlier in this chapter, at this stage we shall look at the factors which the internal analysis might encompass and some of the issues in conducting this part of the audit. As with the environmental analysis, however, the internal analysis is a means to an end and in particular forms the basis for assessing the strengths and weaknesses of the organisation as the second half of the SWOT analysis stage of strategic marketing planning. As with the environmental analysis, therefore, we shall look at how to interpret and use the results of the internal analysis for the SWOT process in Chapter 5. First, we must know what to look for in the internal analysis part of the audit and how to proceed.

Factors in an internal appraisal

As with the appraisal of broad environmental factors, it is difficult and potentially dangerous to be definitive about what factors should be included when conducting an internal appraisal for the purpose of developing strategic marketing plans. As with the environmental factors, we need to identify the most relevant areas and activities in the strategic business unit to appraise. Again, as with environmental factors, the most relevant internal factors will vary between industry, company and individual SBUs. Therefore, the manager must use discretion and judgement in selecting areas to appraise. For example, it would make little sense to include, say, design capabilities in the assessment if this capability is unimportant to customers and hence competitive market success. Herein lies the clue to identifying the relevant internal factors which should be included in the appraisal. Management must first assess which areas of company activity and resources are critical to competitive success. Essentially, the important activities and resources are those which result in outputs which are valued by customers. Again, it is important to assess these activities and resources from the point of view of the external customer or potential customer and not from the internal perspective of

The internal audit of the company's activities and resources should essentially reflect the viewpoint and valuation of the customer.

the company and, as with the appraisal of environmental factors, it is important to avoid a narrow product-based perspective on these.

Ideally, the identification of key activities and resources for appraisal should be carried out by a management team, but for this exercise it may also be useful to include the views of customers to help in the process of identification. It is useful to examine the key factors for success (KFS) in the marketplace – for example, speed of delivery, technical service, competitive prices, and so on, and then to work backwards from these factors to identify which resources and activities underpin them.

Bearing in mind that each company and, as stated, probably each SBU, must identify its own factors to be included in the internal appraisal, it is possible to identify a checklist of factors which contains some of the most likely areas which the internal part of the marketing audit may encompass. Clearly, such checklists need to be used with care and discretion. A possible checklist of factors for internal appraisal is as follows:

Financial

- Gearing.
- Liquidity.
- Profit margins.
- Return on shareholder investment.
- Access to short- and long-term capital.

Personnel

- Managerial experience and expertise.
- Levels of training and education.
- Labour turnover.
- Motivation and attitudes.
- Workforce skills.
- Creativity and entrepreneurial flair.
- Relationships between management and unions.
- Leadership skills.

R & D and design

- Budgets.

- Innovative success.
- Rate of new product ideas.
- Design expertise.
- Technological expertise.

Engineering and production

- Production planning and control systems.
- Degree of automation.
- Quality control procedures.
- Age and profile of plant.
- Flexibility.
- Unit costs of production.
- Supply and procurement.

Marketing

- Market share and standing.
- Brand names.
- Market research and information systems.
- Marketing mix elements.
- Forecasting and planning systems.
- Customer orientation/staff attitudes.
- Company image.
- Customer satisfaction.

These, then, are some of the more important factors which the internal appraisal part of the audit might assess. As mentioned earlier, we shall look at how to translate the results of this appraisal into an assessment of strengths and weaknesses in Chapter 5. But it is important at this stage to stress the following considerations with regard to the internal appraisal and assessment elements.

Organising the appraisal

The appraisal should be conducted either by a cross-functional management team, as suggested for environmental appraisal, or preferably by a team of outside consultants who are likely to be more objective and independent in their appraisal. Some companies have their own specialist auditing teams for conducting internal appraisals.

Clearly, the internal appraisal needs to be as systematic as possible and an integral part of the strategic marketing planning process. Elements of the internal appraisal process may involve ongoing feedback and systems, such as customer tracking studies, and so on.

Techniques of the appraisal

We have seen already that checklists can be useful tools in conducting the internal and external marketing audit. One useful technique of appraisal is to produce these checklists in the form of a questionnaire which can be distributed for completion to the appropriate members of the marketing and management team. A sample of the sorts of questions which can be included on such a questionnaire is shown below:

For your brands, are there any changes in the following that could cause problems or open new opportunities for the organisation in the future?

(a) Technology: materials, components, machines.
(b) Techniques: methods, systems.
(c) Design, promotion, presentation.
(d) Non-controllable variables: the economy, legislation, political activity, and so on.

How many of your brands can be considered poor performance products – that is, low sales and/or low profits.

How are your brands performing on sales year-on-year?

(a) In total value.
(b) By area value.
(c) By quantity sold.
(d) By sales to market segments.

The use of questionnaires in the marketing audit can ensure a systematic approach to the audit and at the same time ensure that individual brand managers, for example, are not avoiding aspects of their brands' performance which may show them in a poor light.

Wherever possible, the marketing audit should be quantified, although this is not always possible or appropriate with, say, some of the key environmental factors.

Another useful technique in the marketing audit of environmental factors is the use of 'scenario analysis'. This involves generating scenarios based on possible developments and changes in the marketing environment. These scenarios can be along the lines of 'what if?' questions. For example, the marketing team can assess the potential impact of environmental developments and changes on the marketing strategies and success of the company. Such scenarios can be based on a range of optimistic, pessimistic and most likely assessments of the actual occurrence of an event or trend. These can then be assessed with regard to how critical these events might be with respect to the survival of the organisation.

Summary

In this chapter we have looked at the first half of the marketing audit, which in turn feeds into the assessment of opportunities and threats. Specifically, we have considered the nature, scope and importance of auditing the marketing environment, and those internal activities and resources which underpin success or failure in the marketplace and which therefore need to be assessed in the development of strategic marketing plans. We have seen that the main problem in this area is the potentially enormous range of factors which might conceivably be considered in the process of conducting a marketing audit. It is for each strategic business unit to determine the most important environmental and internal factors to be considered in the audit. It is also problematical to ensure that the audit is objective enough to form a platform for the development of future marketing plans. For this reason, it is a good idea to use a cross-functional team to conduct a marketing audit and/or an external consultancy. Questionnaires are a useful tool for conducting companywide marketing audits and the technique of scenario analysis has proved to be useful in the auditing process.

Chapter 4
The Marketing Audit (2)

INTRODUCTION

In this chapter we continue the marketing audit step of the strategic marketing planning process, although we will now consider the nature, importance and approaches to analysing customers and competitors. It is important to stress that these analyses should be viewed as part of the total marketing audit – in other words, that the analyses are considered together with the analysis of the broad environment factors and the internal analysis of company resources and operations discussed in Chapter 3. Together, the results from the complete marketing audit feed into the SWOT analysis covered in the next chapter.

CUSTOMER ANALYSIS

It goes without saying that customer analysis should be a central part of strategic marketing planning. In fact, as is now widely accepted, effective marketing and marketing plans must be based around a careful analysis of customers. Having said this, perhaps surprisingly, many companies still pay lip-service to the analysis of customers in their marketing planning. Very often this is due to a feeling of familiarity with customers and their needs, particularly where a company has been supplying particular customers or markets for a long period of time. Clearly, the degree of customer analysis required during the marketing audit does depend upon whether or not strategic marketing plans are being drawn up for new or existing markets. Where a marketer is drawing up plans for entering a market for the first time, more information and research into customers will be required. The approach to customer analysis which we have proposed is based around addressing what we feel to be a number of key questions, the answers to which will enable the marketing planner to develop more effective strategic marketing plans through under-standing customers better. These questions are based on the premise that the marketer is preparing strategic marketing plans for a market which is new to the company and therefore involves the greatest degree of search and analysis of customers. In the case of a company preparing strategic marketing plans for existing markets, it may well be that some of the information pertaining to the questions we have proposed for entering new markets is already known on the basis of past experience. However, as already intimated, it is important not to assume too much about customers even where we have served these customers for a number of years. It is particularly important, as already stressed, not to become complacent about our level of understanding of customers. As with the broader environmental forces and factors discussed in Chapter 3, customers' needs and wants are constantly evolving and changing. Even in the case of preparing plans for existing markets, therefore, it is important to take the opportunity to reassess our customers by addressing the questions we have posed below. The following represent what we feel to be some of the key questions regarding the audit of customers.

Complacency about our knowledge of customers should be avoided in favour of reassessing their needs and requirements through the appropriate research.

Who are the customers?

First, the marketer must assess who are the existing (and potential) customers for the products and services being marketed. Essentially, this means assessing who or what the target market is intended to be. We shall discuss target marketing in some detail in Chapters 6, 7 and 8 but clearly if we are to analyse customers, we must have some notion of who these customers are or are intended to be. Normally, target customers are described using a mixture of customer characteristics, buying needs, lifestyles, and so on. For example, customers (or the target market) might be described as: 'female; socio-economic groups ABC1; age range 25–40; professional/career woman'.

Sometimes, of course, there may be several target customers. As we shall see when we consider targeting, in the case of new markets the marketer must choose who or what the intended customer is to be. However, even in the case of established markets, the marketer must continuously assess if the selected target market is being reached and/or if it needs to be changed.

A further complication in assessing who are the customers is that very often the 'customer' is not the end user or consumer of the product or service. Examples of this are women's perfume or men's shirts and ties. In both of these markets the products are often purchased by someone other than the end user. In the case of women's perfume, for example, often the purchaser is a male buying the product as a gift. Similarly, certainly in the United Kingdom, by far the largest proportion of purchases of men's shirts and ties is made by women on behalf of their partners. It is important, therefore, to distinguish the different roles in the purchasing process when assessing who are the customers. This is important in all markets. In both consumer and business-to-business markets, in fact, we may identify several possible roles in the purchasing process and it is useful for the marketer to understand who fulfils these various roles. The major possible roles in purchasing are outlined below. You will notice both the similarities and the slight differences in the roles between consumer product markets and business-to-business product markets.

Possible roles in consumer purchasing

- *Initiator*: the individual who starts the buying process.
- *Influencer*: the individual who strongly affects the purchase decision.
- *Decider*: the individual who decides any aspect of the purchase process.
- *Buyer*: the individual who makes the purchase.
- *User*: the individual who uses the product or service.

Possible roles in business-to-business purchasing

- *Initiator*: the individual or function who starts the buying process.
- *Gatekeeper*: the individual or function who controls the flows of information and access into and through the buying organisation.

- *Decider:* the individual or function who decides any aspect of the purchase process.
- *Approver:* the individual or function who sanctions any aspect of a purchasing decision.
- *User:* the individual or function who uses the product or service.

Clearly, these roles in both consumer and business-to-business markets may be filled by one or several individuals, but identifying and understanding these different roles can provide valuable insights for developing marketing strategies.

What are the motivations of customers?

A particular important facet of customer analysis is the identification of customer or consumer motivations: What underpins their purchasing decisions? What are their specific needs and wants? How do these change over time?

As mentioned earlier, the understanding of customers' needs through their motives for purchase is central to the marketing concept and can be very powerful in helping to shape strategies. For example, imagine the marketer of a new brand of lager establishing through research that the following are the key motives for purchase:

- ❏ Flavour.
- ❏ Strength.
- ❏ Value for money.
- ❏ Image

Clearly, identifying these key motives will be invaluable in developing, for example, segmentation, targeting, positioning strategies and the marketing mix. Ongoing customer research, and particularly the use of focus groups, is essential in helping to understand customer motives.

Are there any unsatisfied needs?

The process of uncovering customer motives may well lead to the identification of unsatisfied needs in a market. Unsatisfied needs may arise either because customer needs are not being met by existing product offerings and/or because customer are unsatisfied, for a variety of possible reasons, with what is currently being offered. For example, we may find that at least some customers want, and will pay for, better levels of service. Similarly, changing customer needs may give rise to whole new potential markets, as has happened with labour-saving devices and convenience foods as a result of demographic and other social trends. Unmet needs are a prime reason for developing new or improved products. Unsatisfied needs can be monitored through depth interviews but also through consumer panels, problem research and the monitoring of customer complaints and feedback. The presence of unsatisfied needs in a market exposes existing suppliers in that market to the threat of new entrants who are prepared to meet these needs.

How do customers purchase?

This question is concerned with establishing the process of purchasing and includes exploring the following issues:

❑ What steps and stages are involved in the purchase?
❑ Where do customers purchase?
❑ When do customers purchase?

The answers to some of these questions may be relatively straight-forward and already known by the marketer, but the marketer must be careful not to assume too much. Constant appraisal of these areas through research and tracking is essential as they can, and do, change over time. In the case of the marketer who is planning entry into a new market, this information must be sought for the first time and, as for other elements of customer analysis, can provide essential information for developing marketing strategy.

What factors affect purchase and choice?

Finally, in the analysis of customers the strategic marketing planner must understand the main factors which affect purchase and choice. This can be a complex area as so many factors potentially affect purchasing behaviour. Some of these are behavioural in nature – for example, reference groups, lifestyle, personality, and so on. Others are culturally determined, such as social class and, of course, culture itself. Others involve personal factors such as age, occupation, economic circumstances, and so on. All we are suggesting here is that the marketer needs to understand at least the major factors surrounding the purchase in the product market concerned. Again, market research is essential in this area.

COMPETITOR ANALYSIS

The final area in conducting the marketing audit concerns the all-important analysis of competition before the development of strategic marketing plans. In fact, in today's commercial environment one must be as much competitor- as customer-oriented. Another potentially complex area of analysis, auditing competitors can once more be addressed through asking a series of key questions. You will see that competitor analysis involves more than simply assessing existing competitors in a market, but rather extends to assessing the competitive structure of the market.

Who are the competitors?

Understandably, analysing competitors begins with identifying those competitors. As one would expect, in existing markets the marketer probably knows who the main existing competitors are. As with customer analysis, however, it is easy to become blasé. Often new competitors 'creep up' on established companies and it is therefore important to look out for new, even if currently unthreatening, competitors. All too often, though, even (or perhaps especially) companies which have long experience in a market will think of competitors in too narrow a sense. The most obvious competition in a market is usually brand competition – for example, there is no doubting that Pepsi Cola is competing with Coca-Cola. At another level, there is also product class competition – for example, both Pepsi Cola and Coca-Cola are competing with other soft drinks suppliers. Product form competition is where different products essentially supply the same need – for example, 35mm camera marketers are in competition with video camera marketers, and more recently with computer suppliers. Finally, we can argue that all products which compete for a customer's discretionary spending power are in a sense in competition.

Business definition is useful in helping to identify competitors in as much as a major dimension of business definition was customer needs. We should use business definition, therefore, to think about the scope of competition. Companies that are in the 'transport' business are in competition with all other existing and potential suppliers of transport. Related to this, perhaps the most useful way of identifying competition is by analysing customer choices. In particular, it is useful to establish which competitor products the customer considers as potential substitutes when making a purchase and which products are associated with specific use contexts or applications. Ultimately, it is customers, through their choice processes and their notion of substitutes, who determine a company's competitors.

In identifying competitors, it is particularly important to consider potential competitors or at least the extent to which it is easy or difficult for new competitors to enter the market. We should include in our analysis, therefore, an assessment of any new brands, products or technologies which may potentially threaten our markets. We must also assess barriers to entry and, where appropriate, calculate how these barriers may be influenced to make it difficult for competitors to enter.

How intensive is competition?

The second question concerns the intensity of existing or potential competition in a market. Some markets are much more competitive than others, which is important, particularly when assessing new markets. We shall consider this aspect again when we consider targeting in Chapter 7. But in broad terms, markets are generally more competitive where the following conditions exist:

❑ Large numbers of competitors.
❑ Few barriers to entry.
❑ Extensive exit barriers.
❑ Homogeneous products.
❑ Profitable and growing markets.

What are the strengths and weaknesses of competitors?

A key part of competitor analysis is assessing their strengths and weaknesses. Given that the analysis of competitors will be used to shape marketing strategies, and given that we would seek to avoid strategies which expose us to competitors who are stronger than ourselves, it is important to assess their strengths and weaknesses relative to those of our own organisation. In some ways this analysis mirrors the internal analysis of our own organisation's resources, described in the previous chapter, and should encompass the same key areas, but for our competitors rather than for ourselves. For example, the analysis would look at aspects such as financial strengths and weaknesses, relative product quality, delivery performance, share of distribution channels, sales and market growth, and so on. Clearly, this analysis is more problematical when a competitor's profile is being considered simply because of the potential difficulty of having access to accurate information on which to base the analysis. However, several sources of information on competitors may be accessed, for example, through trade information, mystery shopping, distributor feedback, market research studies and published data, such as company reports, promotional material, and so on. Perhaps one of the most useful sources of information on competitors are the views and opinions of customers. Ultimately, it is customer choice which determines the impact of perceptions regarding competitor strengths and weaknesses.

What are our competitors' current and future strategies?

In analysing competitors it is essential to consider how they are currently competing in our markets and, albeit with more difficulty, to assess their possible future strategies. This analysis can provide clues as to how to deal with competitors in a strategic way. For example, if it can be established that a competitor intends to launch a new product, steps can be taken to minimise or to pre-empt the effects of this.

Assess your competitors' strengths and weaknesses in the light of your own organisation's resources and develop strategies to combat their threats to your market.

What are our competitors' reactions likely to be?

Before developing and implementing competitor strategies it is important to try to assess the likely reactions of competitors to any of our moves in the market. For example, some competitors are selective in their responses and may only respond when they are threatened by, say, price cutting. Some competitors may be very aggressive in their reactions to the marketing strategies of opponents, whereas others may only respond if they are directly threatened.

Who or what are likely to be our future competitors?

Markets, and particularly the competitor element, are never static. As far as competitors are concerned, existing ones will disappear and new ones will emerge. Sometimes new competitors come from an unexpected quarter. For example, new technologies may threaten old ones before the unaware marketer has time to respond. As we have seen so often, customers and their changing needs and purchasing patterns may give rise to new competitors. As with the intensity of competition in a market, the potential for new competitors is in large part determined by the existence, or otherwise, of barriers to entry. The marketer must constantly assess, therefore, what these barriers are and how they are changing, if at all. Some of the most important barriers to entry include:

❑ Costs of entry – for example, investment levels.
❑ Extent of differentiation between competitor offerings.
❑ Extent of brand loyalty.
❑ Economies of scale.
❑ Patent and other legal barriers.

Some of these barriers to entry can be affected and shaped by the efforts of the marketer – for example, differentiation and brand loyalty. Clearly, how they are shaped and for what purpose depends to a large extent on whether we are considering a present incumbent of the industry/market or a potential entrant. In any event, barriers to entry are not permanent, but can be influenced by marketing strategies.

Summary

In this second chapter on the marketing audit we have looked at the issues in, and approaches to, analysing customers and competitors. It is important to keep up to date with respect to changing customer needs and how customers purchase. By plotting changes and trends in these areas, it is possible to isolate potential problems and identify marketing opportunities. A series of simple questions regarding customers enables the marketer to identify target customers, the roles in the purchasing process and the factors that affect these. Both consumer and business customer may need to be assessed according to the circumstances. Similarly, we have seen that a key part of the marketing audit is the analysis of competition. We must identify who the competitors are, both existing and potential, the intensity of competition in the industry, competitor strengths and weaknesses, competitor strategies and possible competitor reactions to our strategies in the marketplace.

Chapter 5
The SWOT Analysis

INTRODUCTION

In this chapter we will look at how the elements of the marketing audit, both internal and external, which were discussed in Chapters 3 and 4, are utilised in the development of strategic marketing plans. As already mentioned, the link in moving from the analysis of environmental, market and internal analyses to the use of these analyses in planning is provided by what is commonly referred to as a SWOT analysis. In this chapter, therefore, we consider the process and uses of assessing strengths and weaknesses, and the opportunities and threats in the process of developing strategic marketing plans. This much vaunted but also often misunderstood, and therefore inappropriately applied element, is known by virtually all those concerned with planning by the initial letters of the analysis (hence the term SWOT analysis). In effect, the SWOT analysis is the concluding part of the analysis stage of marketing planning encompassed by the marketing auditing process which was discussed in the previous two chapters, in as much as the purpose of the marketing audit is to produce an assessment of strengths and weaknesses, and opportunities and threats. However, because of the importance of the SWOT analysis in the development of strategic marketing plans, and because the subtleties and complexities of this analysis are often underestimated and/or misunderstood, we have felt it appropriate to devote a separate chapter to this key step in the planning process. We shall start by examining why the SWOT analysis is so important by highlighting its uses and relevance to the development of strategic marketing plans.

THE PURPOSE AND USES OF THE SWOT ANALYSIS

As we have seen in Chapters 3 and 4, the marketer must analyse carefully both the internal and external environment, including customers and competitors, in order to understand the current situation facing the company, and perhaps more importantly, the trends and changes in these internal and external factors which may affect the organisation in the future. The whole purpose of such a wide-ranging and often complex and costly audit, however, is so that the marketer can develop more effective marketing strategies. The mechanism for moving from the information provided through the marketing audit to the use of this information in developing marketing strategies is the SWOT analysis.

Essentially, the SWOT analysis is used to develop strategies which build on identified strengths and avoid or obviate identified weaknesses. An organisation can only build a sustainable competitive advantage by capitalising on its strengths compared to the competitors. But these strengths must match the requirements of the environment and in particular the requirements for competitive success based on customer needs. It is often said that the essence of effective strategic marketing is achieving a strategic fit between the organisation – that is, the strengths and weaknesses – and the environment – that is, the opportunities and threats. Identification of the strengths and weaknesses, and the opportunities and threats, therefore, is central to the development of strategies. We must understand, therefore, how to move from the appraisal stage of the marketing audit, where the key forces and factors, both internal and external to the organisation, are identified, forecast and assessed, to the use of these appraisals in the development of marketing strategies. As mentioned earlier, the mechanism for this movement is the SWOT analysis. But how should the SWOT analysis be conducted and how does it differ from the key elements of the internal and external analysis already conducted?

Identifying and building on the company's strengths while eliminating its weaknesses will help it to maintain a competitive advantage in the marketplace.

PREPARING A SWOT ANALYSIS

The first two stages of the marketing audit should have identified the key environmental factors, and trends and changes in these factors, and the performance and resources of the organisation with respect to internal factors. As already mentioned, we must now move from this stage into an assessment of what are the significant opportunities and threats, and what are the key strengths and weaknesses. A suggested approach to this process is as follows:

❏ First, we need to identify the most important factors in the organisation's environment. Initially, this will involve listing and forecasting the PEST factors, together with the elements of the competitive environment as outlined in Chapters 3 and 4.

❏ Next, these factors must be ranked according to which of them are likely to pose the key opportunities and the key threats. This ranking is best conducted by a management team as outlined in Chapter 3. Inevitably, this ranking process is likely to be subjective. However, as a guide to conducting the ranking process, the following are likely to be key considerations for the management team:

– The most significant factors are those which potentially have the greatest impact on the achievement of organisational corporate and marketing objectives, which in turn is related to the nature of the product markets in which the company operates or intends to operate in the future. For example, a company which manufactures and markets products containing freons such as, say, refrigerators, will be potentially significantly affected by trends and changes which affect the regulation and use of such chemicals. An aid to assessing the significance of trends and changes in environmental factors is to score the various factors according to their potential impact (good or bad) on the company, and the probability of occurrence of the forecast trend or change. For example, potential impact could be scored by the management team on a scale of, say, +5 (a trend or change extremely favourable to the company) to –5 (a trend or change extremely unfavourable to the company). Similarly, the probability of occurrence could be scored between, say, one (little chance of occurring) and ten (almost certain to occur). By combining impact and probability scores, it is possible to assess the most important opportunities and threats.

– One way of thinking about and expressing the range of magnitude of opportunities and threats is as follows:

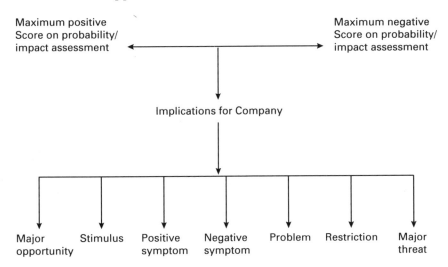

Maximum positive
Score on probability/
impact assessment

Maximum negative
Score on probability/
impact assessment

Implications for Company

| Major opportunity | Stimulus | Positive symptom | Negative symptom | Problem | Restriction | Major threat |

All we are trying to achieve through this process of ranking is some indication of the magnitude of the various opportunities and threats to the company. Clearly, where a numerical approach is taken to the ranking process, it is important not to delude ourselves that in some way the process of assessing the opportunities and threats automatically becomes 'scientific', and the rankings from the process are definitive. As mentioned earlier, the process is still subjective and will require considerable managerial judgement in deciding which are the most important opportunities and threats.

❏ Having identified and appraised the key opportunities and threats, we can now turn our attention to the assessment of the strengths and weaknesses of the organisation. As with opportunities and threats, we must try to identify from what is probably a mass of information from the internal audit appraisal the key strengths and the key weaknesses. Hence, once again we are endeavouring to rank the factors from our internal audit. Using the management team, the following approach is suggested:

– Using the internal resource audit, the team can assess the extent to which the apparent strengths of the company 'match' the opportunities identified in the first stage of the SWOT analysis. Where there is a strong match, we can move from the simple possession of a resource capability towards a true marketing strength.

– Similarly, one must also assess how strong the company is in these areas where there is an apparent match. So, as with the assessment of opportunities and threats, some sort of numerical assessment of strengths and weaknesses can be made. Again, this can be relatively simple using, say, a scale of –5 (major weakness) to +5 (major strength).

– As mentioned in earlier chapters, it is important to remember that resources or skills which have been identified through the marketing audit are only strengths in strategic planning terms if they can be used to advantage in the marketplace. Where this is the case, such resources or skills are sometimes referred to as 'marketing assets'. To qualify as marketing assets, resources or skills must fulfil two key criteria.

First, resources or skills must be of value, or potential value, to the customer and therefore must underpin what were previously referred to as 'key factors for success' in the market (KFS). For example, although a company may be particularly 'strong' in terms of fashion and design, this apparent skill is only a true marketing strength (or marketing asset) where it is sought after and valued by customers. There are plenty of instances where companies, when entering, for example, a new market, have found that what they thought were strengths proved not to be a source of competitive advantage.

Secondly, the resources or skills must be sufficiently superior to those possessed by competitors in the same areas. It is not too difficult to imagine the problems that occur where a company attempts to compete on bases where competitors are superior.

A key part, therefore, of the assessment of strengths and weaknesses, and the interpretation of these with respect to the development of marketing strategies, is the analysis of customers and competitors as outlined in Chapter 4. We shall also see in later chapters that the selection of marketing strategies themselves require this comparison of company strengths and weaknesses with the needs of the market, and the strengths and weaknesses of competitors.

Summary

In this chapter we have looked at one of the most pervasive, important, and yet in some ways least understood elements of strategic marketing planning – namely, the SWOT analysis. This analysis provides the mechanism for moving from the audit and analysis of internal and external factors towards the use of these audits and analyses in the development of marketing objectives and strategies. What the SWOT analysis should enable the strategic marketing planner to achieve is an understanding of the key opportunities and threats faced by the organisation, and how the strengths of the organisation may be used to take advantage of these opportunities, while at the same time obviating any weaknesses and minimising or removing major threats. In later chapters we shall see the significance and uses of the SWOT analysis in selecting between major strategic marketing alternatives. We have suggested how the SWOT analysis can be made systematic even though the process inevitably requires experience and judgement on the part of the strategic marketing planning team.

Chapter 6
Target Marketing (1)

INTRODUCTION

To date we have examined the major inputs to develop the strategic marketing plan, including the analyses required. For example, we have looked at the corporate framework within which strategic marketing plans are developed, including the identification of strategic business units (SBUs) and business definition. We have also examined the key elements of a systematic appraisal encompassing the current situation of a business brought about through the marketing audit, culminating in the preparation of a SWOT analysis for the business. The purpose of delineating the corporate framework and conducting a systematic and thorough marketing audit, however, is that they form the input into the development of the decision-making and action parts of the strategic marketing plan. We are now in a position, therefore, to turn our attention to these key decision and action elements.

We shall begin with what many consider to be among the most important elements of the strategic marketing plan – namely, the interrelated elements of segmentation, targeting and positioning; normally, these three elements are collectively referred to as target marketing. Indeed, these three elements are so central to the development of effective strategic marketing plans that we have devoted this and the next two chapters to a discussion of them. In this chapter we begin with the first element in target marketing decisions – namely, the identification of market segments. In the next two chapters we then discuss the choice of market segments or targeting, and positioning. It is important to stress that these three chapters comprise the individual elements of the overall process of target marketing and should be considered as one process.

THE MEANING AND IMPORTANCE OF MARKET SEGMENTATION

Within virtually all the markets for products and services there are usually different customers who want different things. For example, within the 'car market', there are distinct and different preferences for different types of cars. Some customers will want, and can afford, a larger, more prestigious model; others will be looking for a two-seater sports car perhaps to enhance their image or reputation, yet others will be interested primarily in a mode of transport which is cheap, safe and reliable. Similarly, not all companies which want to purchase computer systems will be looking for the same package. Some will require specific facilities such as computer-aided design, others will be looking for a full system support, including installation, training and maintenance. All this means that within the overall market for a product or service there are usually distinct subsets, clusters, or, as they are normally referred to in marketing, market segments, which within each cluster or segment have similar or homogeneous needs and wants, but which between the different clusters or segments exhibit different needs and wants. A key part of developing strategic marketing plans, therefore, is to determine what these different needs and wants are, and which of the different segments of the market the marketer is intending to cater for, and on what basis. As mentioned earlier, this is a three-step process involving segmentation, targeting and positioning. The segmentation step comprises the identification stage of the process whereby the marketer assesses the market segments and, if so, on what basis.

The start point of target marketing is to recognise and identify the different preferences and needs of different customers.

The importance of the segmentation process, therefore, is that it provides the platform for the targeting and positioning steps which follow. The importance of effective segmentation can be emphasised by highlighting the advantages of target marketing in general and the segmentation part of it in particular. These advantages are as follows:

❏ Segmentation allows a company to identify specific consumer groups which have different needs and wants.

❑ By identifying these different needs and wants the marketer is in a better position to determine which market segments the company is best able to serve.

❑ Segmentation allows both large and small companies to compete more effectively in markets.

❑ Segmentation allows the development of more tailored marketing mixes to the specific needs and wants of the different customer groups.

❑ Segmentation may be used to identify gaps in the market which the company may wish to serve.

❑ Segmentation forces a constant appraisal of changing customer needs and wants, and any potential opportunities and threats which arise therefrom.

The advantages of market segmentation speak for themselves in underpinning the importance of segmentation in particular and target marketing in general. Moreover, it is generally acknowledged that markets, through different customer needs and wants, are becoming more heterogeneous over time, thus giving rise to more fragmented markets than in the past and therefore an even greater need for segmentation. This can be seen in the disadvantages associated with not segmenting markets in today's competitive environment. The disadvantages are as follows:

❑ Competitors can exploit underserved segments and gaps in the market.

❑ It is difficult, if not impossible, to develop an effective marketing mix.

❑ A company can find itself trying to satisfy all the market with a mass-marketing strategy, but in fact satisfying the needs of none of the market segments effectively.

BASES FOR SEGMENTING MARKETS

Market segmentation requires the marketing planner to identify the most appropriate base(s) for segmenting the market. Before we discuss how to apply these different possible bases to the process of segmentation, we need first to be clear about what these possible bases are. In fact, the number of potential bases for segmenting markets is virtually limitless. Any basis for segmenting a market must simply fulfil the criteria which we shall discuss shortly. Having said this, it is possible to describe some of the more frequently used bases of segmenting markets which are used by contemporary marketers. These are outlined briefly below and, for convenience we have divided them into bases for consumer markets and bases for business-to-business markets.

Bases for segmenting consumer markets

❏ *Demographic*: some of the most frequently used bases for seg-
menting consumer markets are the demographic characteristics of consumers. Age, sex, geographical location, marital status, nationality, religion and family size are among the most widely used bases in this category.

❏ *Socio-economic*: in this category, the two most widely used bases are probably income and social class.

❏ *Personality and lifestyle*: personality type and particularly different lifestyles have been increasingly used to identify market segments. Lifestyle segmentation is based on the notion that the attitudes, activities and opinions of different individuals give rise to different purchasing needs and wants. For example, some indivi-
duals' lifestyles are characterised by a search for, say, 'excitement and adventure', whereas others may have a lifestyle characterised by a need for 'security and continuity'.

❏ *Purchase behaviour*: markets may also be segmented around the nature of purchasing behaviour. For example, we may distinguish between, say, 'first time' and 'repeat buyers' or between buyers with different degrees of brand loyalty.

❏ *Consumption behaviour*: some buyers may be 'heavy or frequent users' of a product or service, whereas others may be 'light or infrequent users'. Different types of consumption behaviour may be useful in identifying different segments.

❏ *Combination bases*: in recent years, marketers had moved towards using a combination of elements as a basis for segmenting markets. The elements combined in this way vary between the different systems used, many of which are commercial packages available from market research and advertising agencies. Good examples of such combination bases are the so-called geo-demographic bases such as ACORN, PINPOINT and MOSAIC systems.

Market segmentation can be based more effectively on the different benefits that customers are seeking from a purchase than on consumer characteristics or purchase-related behaviour.

❑ *Benefits sought*: given that all market segmentation is based on identifying different clusters of customers who have similar needs within a segment but different needs across the segments, this implies that different segments are looking for different benefits from the purchase of a product or service. If this is the case, which indeed it is, then it might be appropriate to segment a market directly by identifying the benefits sought by each segment rather than by using indirect attributes such as, for example, consumer characteristics or even purchase-related behaviour. In fact, the factor of the benefits sought by customers underpins all segmentation bases but, as we shall see when we examine the criteria for assessing the different potential bases for segmentation, it may be more problematical in application compared to some of the other bases outlined here.

Bases for segmenting business-to-business markets

❑ Company characteristics – eg, size of company, public versus private, service versus manufacturing.
❑ Geographical location.
❑ Industry/type of application.
❑ Purchase behaviour – for example, centralised versus non-centralised purchasing, new task versus modified or repeat purchase behaviour.
❑ Consumption behaviour – for example, 'heavy' or 'frequent users' versus 'light' or 'infrequent users'.
❑ Benefits sought. As with consumer market segmentation, benefits sought is potentially the most powerful direct form of market segmentation because, as already emphasised, it underpins all market segmentation bases. Here too, though, the application of this basis of segmentation is more problematical than with some of the indirect bases.

These, then, are some of the more commonly found bases for

segmenting markets. We would stress, however, that it is possible to segment a market on any base(s), and you must determine the most appropriate base(s) for your particular product markets. In this context, it is important to understand the criteria for evaluating the different potential bases for segmenting a market. These are outlined below.

EVALUATING POTENTIAL BASES FOR SEGMENTATION

In considering alternative bases for segmenting a market, the following criteria for assessing the different bases should be borne in mind:

❏ *Measurability/identifiability*: ideally, the bases should enable us to identify and measure readily the constituents and characteristics of a segment – for example, how many people are in it, who are they, and so on. For example, the social class of customers in many markets is relatively easy to identify and there are often good secondary statistics which enable us to measure the size of the different segments based on different social class groupings. Some of the other bases for segmenting markets are more difficult to measure and identify, including, for example, 'personality/lifestyle' and 'benefits sought'.

❏ *Accessibility*: ideally, the bases used to segment our markets should enable us to reach those segments through our targeting strategies. For example, segmenting on the basis of, say, age, in most markets, enables us to reach easily the different age groups to be targeted through the different media vehicles. Once again, 'benefits sought' may be more difficult to apply in this respect than some of the other more indirect bases of segmentation.

❏ *Validity*: this is the most important criterion for assessing segmentation bases. What we mean by 'validity' is the extent to which the basis is directly associated with differences in the needs and wants between the different segments. Given that segmentation is essentially about identifying groups with these different needs and wants, it is vital that the segmentation basis is meaningful in this respect. For example, it is pointless to segment a market on the basis of, say, social class, if this basis is not a discriminator between the wants and needs of different groups in the market. Moreover, this discriminatory power of segmentation bases should enable the marketer to predict precisely what these different needs and wants will be, and how and why they will differ between the different segments identified on the basis used. The validity criterion is the reason why 'benefits sought' is potentially the most powerful and useful method of segmenting markets. However, this does not mean that other more indirect bases, which may be easier to identify and measure, may not be useful, and indeed in some instances may be used instead of a benefits sought basis where these other bases are strongly associated with, as a sort of 'proxy' measure, benefits sought. In practice, the application of the segmentation stage of targeting will normally involve the combination of several bases, including both indirect and direct bases in order to arrive at meaningful and useful segments for the purposes of the subsequent stages of targeting and positioning.

APPLYING MARKET SEGMENTATION

Although the precise steps in a market segmentation process may differ slightly according to circumstances, the general approach to this element is as follows:

1. Identify the broad segments in the market based on relevant customer characteristics.
2. Assess the extent to which the market segments identified in the first stage enable us to identify and develop appropriate marketing mixes bases on a clear identification of customer needs in each segment. If at this stage each identified segment is assessed as meeting the criteria identified earlier of measurability, accessibility and validity, then the market segmentation process does not need to be taken further. If, however, our initial broad segmentation does not meet these criteria to our satisfaction, then we may need to segment further.
3. If the relevant criteria for segmentation are not met in the second stage, then we must further segment the broad bases identified

using further bases. This process needs to continue until we are satisfied that the segments identified through the combination of bases used now meet the criteria for selecting market segmentation bases and that they will allow us to proceed to develop targeting strategies on the basis of clearly identified market segments which require different marketing mix programmes.

As throughout the strategic marketing planning process, identifying market segments and the bases on which they are founded will often require marketing research. Both secondary and primary marketing research can be, and are, used in identifying market segments. For example, secondary marketing research may well provide useful information for initial broad segmentation analysis and will often be useful in helping to clarify quantitative aspects of segments such as size, and so on. Primary marketing research, on the other hand, and particularly qualitative research, such as depth interviews and focus groups, are particularly relevant to analysing differences in customer needs, perceptions, benefits sought, and so on.

Summary

In this chapter we have explored the first step in the target marketing process – namely, market segmentation. We have seen that market segmentation is based on the notion that customers have different needs and that the start point of target marketing is identifying these different needs. A variety of bases may be used to segment markets, although some are used more frequently than others. Generally, the bases used to segment consumer and business to business markets differ, although there are some similarities, and in particular the relevance and appropriateness of the so-called 'benefits sought' basis which underpins all market segmentation. We are now in a position to move to the second stage of target marketing – namely, the evaluation of the segments identified so that the marketer may determine which segments are to be selected as target markets.

Chapter 7
Target Marketing (2)

INTRODUCTION

In Chapter 6 we discussed the process of target marketing, including the bases in identifying market segments. In this chapter we shall examine the process of choosing between the different market segments identified by a company. In particular, we shall look at the range of alternative targeting strategies which form such an important part of the overall strategic marketing plan. We shall see that in order to determine targeting strategies it is necessary to evaluate the various market segments with respect to a number of criteria which in effect will enable us to assess which are the most attractive segments to target for our particular company, and also the relative merits of the various targeting strategies available to the marketer.

EVALUATING MARKET SEGMENTS

A number of criteria are important in evaluating the market segments identified in step 1 of the target marketing process, described below. We shall start with those criteria which will help us to make an objective assessment of the inherent attractiveness of a market segment. These are outlined and discussed below.

Market analysis

The first step in evaluating market segments is to analyse the characteristics of the segment itself with regard to a number of key factors as follows:

1. *Market size*: in assessing the attractiveness of a market segment, a good start pointing is to assess the size of the market. This should be measured in both volume and value terms. The size of the market provides a ball-park figure which enables the marketer to begin to assess the potential sales value of a market segment. Clearly, if sales targets are set in terms of the percentage market share, it makes a big difference according to what the size of the market actually is. The problems of estimating the market size differ according to whether this is a new or an existing market. In the case of an existing market, the size can be estimated using a variety of sources, such as government and trade publications, information on competitor sales, and so on. In the case of a potential new market, estimating the market size can be more problematical and will usually require primary research based on surveying potential customers. A key question that arises with respect to the market size concerns the issue as to whether a larger market is always necessarily more attractive as a segment than a smaller one. Clearly, there is no simple answer to this. For example, a larger market potentially allows volume sales but at the same time is also likely to attract more competitors. Similarly, a small company may be at a distinct disadvantage where the market segment is large.

2. *Market dynamics* (for example, potential growth product life cycle): in addition to assessing the current size of a market segment, particularly when considering the decision about whether or not to enter a new segment, we are likely to be as, if not more, concerned about the future size of the market segment. More broadly, we must assess and understand the dynamics of a market segment. By dynamics we mean the factors that drive a market segment and which will determine its growth or contraction in the future. For example, we need to understand at what stage the market segment is with respect to, say, the product life cycle; clearly, segments which are at the introductory or growth stages of the life cycle are very different in terms of overall attractiveness compared to segments which are in the maturity or decline stages. In addition to the dynamics of the market we must also assess any growth potential which is currently unrealised in the segment. For

example, the current size of the market might be only a fraction of the potential market if new uses or users can be addressed through our marketing.

Once again, what constitutes an attractive market segment with respect to the dynamics involved varies according to the situation. For example, some companies are only interested in segments which have the potential for future growth because, say, they are at an early stage of the product life cycle. However, segments can also be very attractive, even to new entrants, when they are at the decline stage. Often at this stage large competitors exit the market, leaving profit opportunities for those companies which are prepared to supply the tail-end of demand.

There is the potential for profit opportunities whether a company is growing or in decline: understanding market dynamics enables this potential to be achieved.

In understanding market dynamics, both primary and secondary marketing research may be necessary, together with the tools and techniques of forecasting. Of course, predicting the turning points in the dynamics of a market such as, for example, the point at which sales will begin to decline in the life cycle is notoriously difficult, but some estimate does need to be made regarding the overall pattern which the market segment is likely to take.

3. *Key factors for success* (KFS): this element of market analysis requires us to assess the ingredients of success in a market segment. Usually these ingredients, which we refer to as key factors for success, will differ between segments in identifiable and predictable ways. For example, in the luxury car market, the key factors for success include: strong brand image and reputation; effective dealer network and back-up services; professional sales staff. In most market segments the key factors for success will comprise a relatively small number of ingredients – usually, half-a-dozen or so key factors account for success in a market segment.

4. *Competitive structure*: as we saw in Chapter 4, competitor analysis is a key part of strategic marketing planning. In the context of evaluating market segments, it is important to undertake a segment-by-segment analysis of the competitive market structure within each segment along the lines already indicated in our earlier chapter. For example, we need to evaluate the nature and extent of competition in the market segment; the strengths and weaknesses of individual competitors in the segment; the competitive

structure in the segment, including the bargaining power of buyers and suppliers, and the ease of entry and exit to the market segment. Segments which are otherwise potentially very attractive with respect to, say, size and growth, are relatively unattractive when considered from a competitive structure viewpoint.

5. *Profitability analysis*: perhaps in some ways a function of all the other elements which comprise market analysis, ultimately – at least for many companies – the key factor in assessing a market is its existing and potential profitability. For example, the profitability of a market segment is affected by its size, its dynamics, its competitive structure, and so on. Overall, taking into account all of these elements, we must make an assessment of how profitable each segment is likely to be.

Matching market analysis to company analysis

We have looked at the broad characteristics of a market segment which must be evaluated and understood in moving towards the selection of target segments. However, what ultimately decides the attractiveness, or otherwise, of a market segment to a particular company is the extent to which these characteristics match, or can be made to match, the characteristics of the company, and in particular the strengths and weaknesses of the company compared to the requirements for competitive success in the segment. We have already examined the importance of evaluating these strengths and weaknesses through the marketing audit in earlier chapters. The results of this audit should now feed into targeting decisions, resulting in the selection of target markets which best match the company's strengths. Clearly, target market selection must also reflect broader considerations, such as overall corporate objectives and constraints, the importance of which were outlined earlier. The outcome of market and company analysis should be a clear prioritisation of segment attractiveness. Before we move to the selection of specific target segments, however, we must understand and have decided on the targeting strategies which are to be employed in the organisation. These are now discussed in the next section.

TARGETING STRATEGIES

The evaluation of the relative attractiveness of the different market segments which have been identified forms the basis of selecting target segments. However, we will still need to determine both the number of segments to be targeted, and our overall targeting strategy. We can distinguish between three types of targeting strategies.

Undifferentiated targeting strategies

An undifferentiated targeting strategy, as the term suggests, is where we decide in effect to ignore the segmentation in the market (remember that virtually all markets do segment) and choose instead to offer one standard marketing mix to the whole of the market. This approach is also referred to as mass marketing. But if markets do segment (remember that the essence of these segments is that customers in them have different needs and wants), does it make sense for any marketer to pursue a marketing strategy which ignores this segmentation? The answer to this question is virtually always 'no'. It does not usually make good marketing sense to pursue undifferentiated marketing. In the previous chapter we outlined the advantages which accrue from market segmentation and the dangers associated with not identifying market segments. Certainly, at one time it was possible, and indeed necessary, to pursue a mass-marketing strategy during a time when consumer needs were relatively simple and unsophisticated, and where customers were happy simply to be able to buy the product or service. For example, in the early days of the car industry, we know that Henry Ford's undifferentiated marketing strategy of providing any car 'so long as it is black', to the market was, at least initially, very successful. Certainly, in the markets of developed economies, as already discussed, consumer demand is much too fragmented for this approach to work. Having said this, undifferentiated marketing can be appropriate in markets which are characterised by an excess of demand over supply – for example, in some of the previously Communist countries of Eastern Europe, or in other developing countries of the world. This is primarily because the major advantage of undifferentiated targeting

Mass marketing ignores the segmentation whereby customers are differentiated by their individual needs and requirements.

strategies are the lower costs associated with both production and marketing; indeed, this is why the strategy was so successful in the early days of the Ford Motor Company. Undifferentiated marketing allows for greater economies of scale and experience curve effects, and hence potentially lower prices. Even in more differentiated demand conditions, therefore, we should always be careful to consider the relatively lower costs of mass marketing against the potentially increased revenue to be gained through differentiated marketing strategies.

Differentiated targeting strategies

As suggested by the term, differentiated targeting is based on targeting the different segments in the market but with a different, tailored, marketing mix for each. We may decide to target all of the market segments identified or perhaps select several of what we assess to be the most attractive, given our earlier analysis.

The benefit of this approach to targeting is that, being essentially customer oriented, as indicated by the tailoring of each marketing mix to fit more closely the precise needs of each market segment, increased revenue and possibly market share may result. The disadvantage of this approach, as you will no doubt already have gleaned, is the potential loss of the economies of scale in both production and marketing, and hence higher costs. Although this is a very marketing-oriented approach, a balance needs to be stuck. Some companies decide to pursue differentiated targeting but with a certain degree of specialisation. For example, a company marketing temperature measurement devices may decide to target only scientific and medical applications for its devices, while at the same time having different targeting strategies for the subsegments within these broad categories.

Concentrated targeting strategies

Sometimes also referred to as niche marketing, this targeting strategy is based on selecting a very small number of segments – and sometimes only one – as a target market. This targeting strategy is particularly appropriate for the smaller company, with more limited resources. By doing so, a company is able to develop specialist skills and expertise, and build a reputation in its chosen market segment. It also means that many of the costs associated with differentiated marketing are avoided. By far the biggest disadvantage of concentrated targeting, though, is the fact that niche marketers are very vulnerable to threatening changes or developments in their markets. For example, should a large competitor choose to enter the market, or if tastes change and the product being marketed goes out of fashion, there will be no other markets to fall back on. Having said this, in the business which has several SBUs, we may practise concentrated targeting in one or more parts of the business and still have other markets to fall back on should an individual SBU find itself threatened.

By selecting a target market, niche marketing has the advantage of specialised skills and lower costs, but the disadvantage of having no other markets to fall back on.

Summary

In this chapter we have explored the second step in the target marketing element of strategic marketing planning. In order to determine appropriate targeting strategies, it is necessary to evaluate the market segments identified earlier. Several broad criteria are usually relevant to this evaluation, including, for example, market size, growth, competitive structure, and so on. In addition, we must assess the attractiveness or otherwise of the segments from the perspective of the company's particular strengths and weaknesses, and its overall corporate and marketing objectives. Having evaluated market segments, the marketer must then select the most appropriate targeting strategies from the alternatives of either undifferentiated (mass) marketing, differentiated marketing, or concentrated (niche) marketing. Having made this choice, we may now to turn to the third and final step in target marketing – namely, positioning.

Chapter 8

Target Marketing (3)

INTRODUCTION

In this Chapter we consider the final element in the process of target marketing. In Chapter 6 we looked at the notion of segmentation and the different bases for segmenting markets. In Chapter 7 we looked at the evaluation aspects of market segments and the range of targeting statistics. Having segmented and selected target markets, the final step in this part of strategic marketing planning involves ensuring that products and services reach selected target segments, and are perceived by customers in a manner which is predetermined and planned for by the marketer and which is designed to give a competitive market edge. This process of reaching target segments and ensuring the right perceptions about a product or service is referred to as positioning, and is one of the most important elements of contemporary marketing. Positioning effectively forms the basis of developing detailed marketing mix plans, around which in turn we can develop sales plans, budgets and controls. In the process, positioning indicates to the market what the product or service stands for, and enables customers to evaluate the offering against competitors.

AN EXPLANATION OF POSITIONING

If we imagine that the strategic marketing plan we are developing concerns a company which is launching a new brand into an established market, and that the marketer has identified the different market segments and selected a target market, then the next step is to ensure that the new brand is positioned into the targeted segment,

Careful, predetermined positioning of a new brand in a selected target market will ensure a competitive edge within the market.

and within this segment it is positioned in a manner which has been predetermined by the marketer in order to ensure a competitive edge. But how can the marketer achieve this two-pronged positioning objective?

The easiest way to explain how this can be achieved is to examine the steps in the process for positioning our hypothetical brand. These steps are as follows:

1. Establish the relevant attributes which are used by customers in the segment when evaluating and choosing between brands in this market.
2. Using these attributes, assess the current perceived position of existing brands in the market, where appropriate, using techniques such as perceptual/brand mapping.
3. Determine where the new brand is to be positioned against existing brands in the market and the brand attributes which will be stressed in order to achieve this position.

We shall now examine each of these steps in more detail.

Establishing relevant attributes

In the first step, we are seeking to establish the key dimensions or attributes of a brand within the market segment in which we are interested which are salient to customer choice. For example, in the cigarette market we may find that among the key attributes of brand choice are: taste; strength; price; image.

We can establish these dimensions through both qualitative and quantitative research. In fact, marketers and market researchers have developed a number of very powerful techniques for identifying the key attributes of choice in markets. A relatively simply method is based on asking a sample of customers to assess the extent of similarity/dissimilarity between competing brands and then uncovering, through focus group interviews, the bases for these judgements. Given that often there are multiple attributes in brand choice, we also need to uncover which are the most important in the choice process.

Establishing perceived positions of existing brands against the key attributes of choice

Once we have determined which brand attributes are most salient to customers when they evaluate and choose between brands, we can then assess where existing brands in the market are perceived to be with respect to these attributes. A very useful technique for achieving this assessment is through the use of perceptual brand maps. A simple example of this type of mapping technique is shown in the figure below. For continuity, let us assume that the map is for the cigarette market. For the purpose of the exercise, let us assume that our qualitative and quantitative research has shown that the two major dimensions in brand evaluation and choice have been found to be 'strength' and 'price/image'. We have then asked our sample of customers to assess where they perceive current brands to be with respect to these two dimensions. Each circle in Figure 8.1 represents a hypothetical perceived position for each of the existing brands in the market. In other words, this technique allows us to map the perceived position of competing brands with respect to the key dimensions of choice. We can now use this type of information to develop the appropriate positioning strategies for our proposed new brand.

Perceptual maps are a useful means of assessing the customer's perceived position of competing brands.

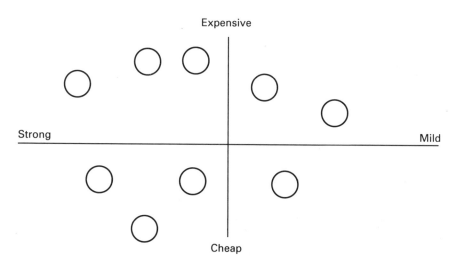

Figure 8.1   A simple perceptual brand map: the cigarette market

Developing a positioning strategy for the new brand

A number of alternative positions are possible for the new brand. Broadly, the brand may be positioned as essentially being either predominantly 'strong and expensive', or 'strong and cheap', or 'mild and expensive', or 'mild and cheap'.

Which of these alternatives, if any, is the most appropriate for the new brand depends on a number of factors. For example, we must assess the relative size of the markets for the different types of products. Similarly, we must assess the relative strengths of the existing competitive brands in the market and whether we would wish to position our brand in direct competition against them or not. Finally, we must assess what our objectives are for the new brand, not only with respect to sales and market share but also in terms of, for example, preferred company and brand image.

Needless to say, this is very much a simplified description of the process of developing positioning strategies for a new brand, but it does illustrate the notion of positioning which is based on the determinant attributes of choice and customer perceptions. In fact, positioning research and techniques, although somewhat more complex in application than is suggested here, are potentially very powerful in developing effective competitive marketing strategies. For example, the technique can be used to look for gaps in markets where current brands appear not to be positioned. Similarly, by exploring the notion of the characteristics of an 'ideal brand' we can develop brands which are nearer to such an 'ideal' and hence attempt to capture relatively dissatisfied customers from other brands.

It is important to note that positioning is achieved through the planning and implementation of the elements of the marketing mix, and this, therefore, is its importance in the overall process of developing strategic marketing plans. Clearly, product, price, place and particularly promotion decisions need to be configured around, and based upon, positioning strategies for a brand.

Our simplified example illustrates positioning a new brand based on brand attributes. However, this is only one approach to implementing positioning. There are, in fact, numerous ways to position brands. For example, a brand may be positioned with respect to particular uses or applications. We might position a shampoo, for instance, as primarily a medicated product for use with problems such as dandruff etc. Alternatively, a brand may be positioned by associating it strongly with a particular user or class of users – for example, a shampoo might be positioned as being predominantly for use by children. A third example of positioning is where a brand is positioned with regard to a particular product class – for example, some shampoos are positioned as 'professional' rather than as 'household' products.

Finally, a positioning strategy may deliberately position a brand with respect to a competitor. Often, although not always, with a new brand the competitor chosen to position against may well be the market leader. One of the best known examples of this was in the car rental market where Avis deliberately positioned themselves with respect to the market leader Hertz by stressing the fact that because they were number two in the market, they tried harder to serve customers.

POSITIONING AND EXISTING BRANDS: REPOSITIONING

In explaining the notion of positioning and the basis of how it works, we have used the example of developing and launching a new brand into an existing market, although obviously not all marketing strategy centres on new brands. The concepts and techniques of positioning already outlined in this chapter are, in fact, also relevant and useful to the development of strategic marketing plans for existing brands. Continuous positioning research into existing brands is essential in order to track, for example, changes in customer choice determinants, changes in customer perceptions of brands, new competitors, and so on. Sometimes this research may suggest that brand positioning is still effective and that no changes in positioning strategies are required. As we know, however, markets are dynamic and this means that for various reasons it may be necessary to consider repositioning strategies for existing brands.

Again, as with the initial positioning itself, repositioning may be achieved through a wide variety of possible strategies. The nature and

Repositioning existing brands is necessary to counter the demands of an ever-changing market.

effectiveness of these various strategies will depend, to a large extent, upon the reasons underpinning the need to reposition. These could include, for example, changes in competitor activity, changes in customer needs and tastes, changes in legislation pertaining to the brand, and so on. Some of the more frequently encountered objectives and strategies for repositioning, however, are outlined below.

Repositioning with existing customers

This type of repositioning is most frequently done in order to revitalise a flagging brand by giving it a new or improved personality. This may be required because, for example, competitor brands in the market have been updated and are more fashionable and hence competitive, or because customers' needs and wants have changed over time and the brand needs to be repositioned to meet these requirements. Often repositioning of this nature is done in order to maintain a brand while a new product is being developed. Another reason for possibly having to reposition a brand with existing customers is where there has been a problem with the brand in the marketplace. For example, a product safety scare or another type of public relations disaster, such as that experienced by Perrier with its table water in the early 1990s.

Sometimes this repositioning may require no more than a change of image, although in the case of a well-known brand, we must not underestimate the cost of image repositioning. A good example of a brand which has changed its image in recent years is Oxo cubes which has had to develop a more contemporary approach to it advertising. In other cases, repositioning may require changes to the product itself or at least to its packaging. An interesting recent example of this is the massively expensive repositioning of the Pepsi Cola brand.

Repositioning to secure new customers

Although repositioning in an existing market may in itself attract new customers, another type of repositioning is where the company deliberately repositions a brand by essentially developing a completely new marketing approach which may involve significant changes to one or more of the marketing mix elements. This is done in order to attract a different type of customer from that attracted previously by the brand. A good example of this is Lucozade. For many years promoted as a brand for the sick and infirm, falling market share and sales required a drastic change of direction for the drink. Gradually, the brand was repositioned first as a pick-me-up for the tired housewife, and then as a drink for the younger health-and-fitness segment of the market. This repositioning has been achieved primarily through promotion and brand image and, like the Oxo example, has been a gradual process involving considerable promotional expenditure. Sometimes repositioning to secure new customers may require drastic changes to the product itself.

The problem with repositioning to attract new customers is that, for obvious reasons, often we lose (sometimes deliberately) the previous customers for the brand. It can be very difficult, though, to convince new customers that the brand has indeed changed. Sometimes it may be better to start from scratch with a completely new brand.

Sometimes we can reposition a brand by stressing different ways in which the product may be used by customers. For example, Johnson's baby products have extended their market by stressing that their brands may be used in different ways and by different customers from those originally envisaged.

Innovative repositioning: creating new brand choice attributes

Occasionally, it is possible to create a unique position in a market for a brand by introducing novel ways of positioning the product against competition. One way of achieving this is to create brands which are uniquely strong with respect to some attribute(s) which customers have not used before in brand choice in the market. A good example of this were those brands in the 1970s and 1980s which stressed their 'green' credentials. Of course, approaching positioning by stressing new criteria of brand choice for customers can be both risky and expensive. It often requires the marketer of the brand to 'educate' customers with regard to the importance of the new attributes in choice. However, it can be a very effective way of positioning ahead of competitors.

Competitor depositioning

Finally, somewhat controversially, another strategy as regards positioning is to alter the perceived position of competitive brands in customers' eyes. Clearly, this normally means repositioning competitor brands in a less favourable light. Once frowned upon, even in the harsh commercial world of business, increasingly companies use, for example, comparative advertising and promotion to try to convince customers that their brand is superior. In one sense, of course, there is nothing wrong with this, but the focus of such campaigns has become increasingly pointed and direct regarding the actual, or claimed, limitations of competitors brands.

Competitor depositioning, particularly where it is based on public denigration of competitor brands through promotion, can be extremely dangerous from a legal viewpoint. Often such depositioning is achieved 'at a distance' by subtle and often veiled comparisons of competitor brands. For example, Fairy Liquid advertising effectively attempts to deposition competitors by showing competitor brands, admittedly unnamed, as being inferior with regard to strength and hence value for money.

Summary

In this third and final chapter on target marketing we have covered the crucial area of positioning. Positioning effectively informs customers what the brand stands for and how it differs from competitors' products. Positioning is important both for new and existing brands. With a new product we must ensure that the brand is perceived against competition in a manner which enables the marketer to develop the most effective competitive edge. Over time, existing brands will need repositioning as customers and markets change.

Positioning is central to the development of marketing plans in that effective positioning is achieved by using the elements of the marketing mix. This is true of both consumer goods and also in business-to-business markets. Without a clearly defined targeting and positioning strategy, it is impossible to develop effective marketing mix variables.

Chapter 9
Marketing Strategies (1)

INTRODUCTION

In this and the following chapter we shall look at the strategic alternatives which are available to the marketer and how these various alternatives may be identified, evaluated and selected. In other words, we shall look at strategic choice. In this chapter we shall start by looking at the range of possible strategic objectives which the marketer may pursue and the alternative broad directions or strategies which the marketer may select in order to achieve these objectives. In the following chapter we shall look at the various strategic alternatives for achieving a sustainable competitive advantage in order to achieve the objectives set. One of the major difficulties in this area of the strategic marketing plan is that the full range of strategic alternatives available to a company is virtually unlimited and extremely complex. In an effort to reduce this variety and complexity to manageable proportions, a number of conceptual frameworks which have proved themselves valuable in this respect are used in both this and the following chapter to help us to delineate and discuss the choice between strategic options. In this chapter we shall use three alternative conceptual frameworks which have proved to be useful in delineating between alternative strategic objectives and directions. We shall start by examining what is probably one of the earliest, and in some ways the simplest, if not the most controversial, of models for delineating strategic alternatives – namely, the so-called product life cycle concept. We shall then turn our attention to a model which uses the concept of product market scope which was first proposed by Ansoff. Finally, we shall use the Boston Consulting Group's product portfolio matrix in order to explore strategic alternatives. In the next chapter we shall concentrate on Michael Porter's notion of generic competitive strategies in order to explore the alternative ways of competing in markets with a view to achieving a sustainable competitive advantage. It is important to stress that these conceptual frameworks represent a small selection of those which are available to the contemporary marketer who wishes to develop marketing strategies. It is neither appropriate nor feasible in this text to include all of these frameworks so we have selected those which we feel have proved to be the most useful and robust in terms of helping to develop strategic marketing plans for the practising marketing manager. There are several excellent texts which deal with a more comprehensive set of frameworks in a more academic style than that felt to be useful here.

THE PRODUCT LIFE CYCLE CONCEPT

One of the earliest and best known conceptual frameworks in marketing planning is the product life cycle concept. As the name implies, this concept is based on the notion that all products and services have finite lives. In addition, during this life it is suggested that products pass through a number of distinct stages. The four basic stages found in most descriptions of the product life cycle are:

❏ Introduction.
❏ Growth.
❏ Maturity.
❏ Decline.

These stages, together with a suggested shape of the sales life cycle associated with each stage, are suggested as being typically S-shaped, as shown in Figure 9.1 below.

The product life cycle framework has several suggested uses with regard to marketing planning. However, for our purposes we are interested in the use of the product life cycle for identifying alter-

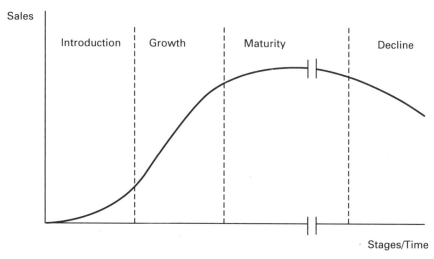

Figure 9.1   The product life cycle framework

native strategic choices. It is suggested that at each of the different stages of the product life cycle certain strategies are likely to be most appropriate. The characteristics of each stage of the life cycle, together with the suggested alternative strategies for each stage are outlined below.

> The product life cycle concept enables marketing strategies to be identified by viewing the product on its four stages of life.

❑ *Introductory stage*: as the name suggests, this is the first stage in the life cycle of a product or market and, as Figure 9.1 shows, is characterised by relatively slow growth in the sales of the product as the market is first developed. Not surprisingly, this stage is critical to future success and in fact many new products never make it past this stage. At this stage there are likely to be few competitors and costs are likely to be high. The suggestion is that heavy promotional expenditures are likely to be needed in order to inform potential customers and to induce trial. According to market and other conditions, a strategy of either charging high initial prices called 'market skimming pricing' or charging relatively low initial prices called 'market penetration pricing' may be used.

❑ *Growth stage*: at this stage sales rise rapidly, as indeed do profits. Competition will start to enter the market and will gradually increase. Strategies during this stage should focus on building the market share and continuing the accelerating sales of the product. Even at this stage the company may need to look to improving product quality and adding new product features. If a high initial skimming price has been used, prices will need to be lowered to expand the market.

❏ *Maturity stage*: at this stage sales begin to peak and start to decline. Profits may decline even more rapidly. A characteristic of this stage is intense competition as competitors fight for a share in a market where sales are slowing. Often special promotional deals will be required at this stage to try to tempt further buyers and above all to build and maintain brand and dealer loyalty.

❏ *Decline stage*: at this stage sales are definitely on a downward spiral as a product or market enters its twilight. Suggested strategies at this stage include, for example, cutting prices, product updates and dealer promotions. Eventually, the marketing manager will have to assess when the product should be withdrawn from the market, with possibly new ones being introduced to replace it.

The product life cycle therefore suggests alternative strategies according to the stage at which a product or market is situated. As you are probably aware, the product life cycle has become somewhat unfashionable as a planning tool, in part at least because of a number of criticisms regarding the concept. For example, some suggest that the concept is too simplistic and that many products do not exhibit the class S-shaped curve which we have discussed. Similarly, some suggest that products do not have 'natural' life cycles at all and that the concept can be dangerous because it becomes a self-fulfilling prophecy.

There is no doubt that there are limitations to the product life cycle concept, but the view taken here is that, used with care and judgement, the concept does still provide potentially useful insights into the development of alternative marketing strategies. Partly because of the criticisms of the product life cycle concept, however, a number of more complex alternative conceptual frameworks of strategic choice have been developed, including the ones we have selected to outline here.

Our second strategic marketing planning tool for developing marketing objectives and strategies is the notion of product market scope.

THE PRODUCT MARKET SCOPE MATRIX

This extremely popular framework (often termed Ansoff's matrix) for delineating alternative marketing strategies has been used for several years now, particularly by those companies with growth objectives. This deceptively simple framework is based on a matrix comprised of 'markets' on the vertical axis and 'products' on the horizontal axis. In turn, each axis is subdivided into 'existing' and 'new'. Each cell of the matrix so formed represents a different strategic alternative for achieving growth. The matrix and each alternative is shown in Figure 9.2.

The simple framework of the product market scope matrix is a useful aid to delineate the range of strategic marketing options.

	PRODUCT	
MARKET	Present	New
Present	1. Market penetration	3. Product development
New	2. Market development	4. Diversification

Figure 9.2 The product market scope matrix

We now turn to each of the strategic alternatives in the matrix:

❑ *Market penetration*: this strategy is based on expanding sales from existing products in existing markets. Where the total market is still growing, this strategy may be achieved, for example, through 'natural market growth'. In markets which are static or declining, however, a market penetration strategy can only be achieved by increasing the market share at the expense of competitors. Clearly, such a strategy will require aggressive marketing backed by, for example, heavy price discounts, promotional activity, and so on.

❑ *Market development*: this strategy is based on expansion by entering new markets but with existing products. For example, the company might attempt to identify additional channels of distribution; alternatively, the company might look for new locations, such as export markets.

❑ *Product development*: this entails developing and launching new products for sale in existing markets. In fact, these might be extensions to the existing product range, such as products with additional features, different packaging, different quality levels. At the other extreme, this strategy may be based on entirely new products for the market. Even where a company is familiar with the market through experience, this can be a risky strategy.

❑ *Diversification*: this strategy is probably the highest risk of all the four strategic options in as much as it involves a company seeking to expand on the basis of new products and new markets. Diversification can take a number of forms – for example, a company may choose to diversify into new product markets that are similar in some way to existing products in that they have some relationship to existing technological and/or marketing know-how but which target new customer groups. The most radical, and therefore the most risky form of diversification growth is where the company diversifies into entirely new products and markets which are unrelated in any way to the existing business. This so-called 'conglomerate' form of diversification was very popular during the 1980s and early 1990s but, because of its attendant risks, has forced companies to be more wary of this method of strategic growth.

This framework is simple to understand but useful in helping to delineate the range of strategic options. Of course, what it cannot do, nor is it intended to do, is to evaluate and choose between the various strategic alternatives. Clearly, strategy selection will depend on a wide range of factors, many of which are outlined elsewhere in this text – for example, strengths and weaknesses assessments, competitor considerations, and so on.

We shall now turn to our third strategic planning framework – namely, the Boston Consulting Group's product portfolio matrix.

THE BOSTON CONSULTING GROUP'S PRODUCT PORTFOLIO MATRIX (BCG MATRIX)

Needless to say, this framework for identifying strategic marketing options was developed by the Boston Consulting Group in America. It was, in fact, when first developed, a pioneer of what have since been termed 'portfolio tools' of strategic market planning. Although one of the first in this field, with other suggestedly more 'refined', more 'useful', but certainly more complex portfolio planning tools having been developed since the so-called BCG matrix, it is still useful and therefore popular, despite many criticisms.

The essentials of the product portfolio matrix are shown in Figure 9.3. The matrix is constructed on the basis of two principal axes – namely, 'relative market share' and 'market growth rate'. Based on these two dimensions the marketer can analyse strategic business units with a view to establishing the balance of the business as a whole and strategies for each business unit according to its position in the matrix. Each business unit is positioned in the matrix according to its relative market share compared to that of the next largest competitor, and the rate of growth in the market of that particular business unit. As can be seen, each axis is split into 'high' and 'low' categories for

The BCG matrix is a useful tool for analysing strategic business units and developing marketing strategies for each one.

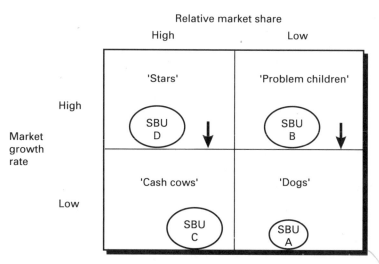

Figure 9.3   The BCG matrix

both market share and market growth. As a rule-of-thumb, anything less than ten per cent market growth rate falls into the low category, and any rate of growth above this falls into the high category. The division between high and low market share cells is that a company must have the highest market share for it to be allocated to the high market share cells. The relative size of the circles for each SBU in Figure 9.3 denotes the relative turnover of each SBU in the business. According to where they lie in the matrix, SBUs are classified as being either 'dogs', 'cash cows', 'problem children', or 'stars'.

The somewhat picturesque technology used for SBUs in the matrix is useful, in fact, in understanding what each cell means. A brief description is given below:

- ❑ 'Dogs' are SBUs with low market share and slow market growth. These products are sometimes referred to as 'cash traps' in that they do not generate a significant cash flow to a company and what little is generated is normally required to be reinvested simply to maintain sales of the product.
- ❑ *'Cash cows'* are SBUs with a high market share and slow market growth. This combination typically means that products in this category generate large amounts of cash over and above that required to keep the product in this sector.
- ❑ *'Problem children'* (also referred to as 'wildcats' and 'question marks') are SBUs with a low market share but in high growth markets. These products can consume cash resources at alarming rates. The overall net drain on cash with these products is greatest when a company attempts to increase its market share.
- ❑ *'Stars'* are SBUs in high growth markets with a relatively high share of the market. Stars can generate relatively large cash inflows, but this is more often than not matched or exceeded by the outflow of cash necessary to maintain the market share. In net terms, therefore, such products provide, at best, modest net cash flows and are often net cash users.

In using and interpreting the product portfolio, a number of factors are important, the first of which is that the portfolio is dynamic – that is, in the absence of any action on the part of a company, SBUs will move their position in the portfolio. Principally because of the product life cycle effect, SBUs have a tendency to move downwards in the portfolio – that is, problem children become dogs and stars become cash cows. This tendency is indicated by the arrows in the figure.

The second factor to note is that the aim is to achieve a certain balance in the portfolio. A balanced portfolio would ideally contain few or no dogs, some problem children, some stars and some cash cows. The balance between problem children, stars and cash cows should ensure that the company has sufficient net positive cash flow from its cash cows to fund the stars which it currently has and turn them eventually into cash cows. Funds from cash cows are also used to turn SBUs which are currently problem children, because of the relatively low market share, into stars. Not all problem children can be moved in this way and eventually some of them will fall to become dogs. In the long run, all dogs are potential candidates for elimination from the product range.

As a consequence of these two factors, a company must take steps to ensure that the future portfolio mix is as the company wishes it to be. In other words, it must select appropriate strategies in order to achieve a future, balanced portfolio.

Four alternative strategies are available:

1. *Build*: the objective is to increase the SBU's market share. This is suitable for question marks in order to turn them into stars.
2. *Hold*: the aim is to maintain the SBU's market share. Holding is appropriate for strong cash cows if they are to continue to make money.
3. *Harvest*: the objective is to increase the short-term cash flow regardless of the long-term effect. This is used with question marks and dogs and also with weak cash cows whose future looks uncertain.
4. *Divest*: the aim is to liquidate or sell the SBU because resources are being wasted on it. This is suitable for dogs and question marks that are draining away the company's profits.

This technique, like most other marketing models, has several problems and limitations which are outlined below.

❏ *Over-simplification*: many critics have argued that the BCG matrix is an over-simplification of product markets and can lead to insufficient management attention to the range of factors which are important in the marketing strategy. For example, the matrix is based on only two key factors – market growth and relative market share.

❑ *Problems of classification*: there are severe conceptual and practical problems associated with defining what comprises a strategic business unit, a concept which is essential to the analysis. Similarly, there is some doubt as to precisely where the line should be drawn between what contributes to a high/low relative market share, and what constitutes high/low market growth.

❑ *Assumptions*: in common with all the strategic portfolio approaches, the BCG model is derived from a number of key underpinning assumptions. If these assumptions are misplaced or wrong, then the subsequent value of the technique is reduced or removed completely. For example, a central assumption of the BCG matrix is that higher rates of market share are associated with higher profit rates. While there is some considerable evidence to support this assumption, it is by no means invariably the case that a higher share equals higher profits.

❑ *Application*: the BCG approach implies that different SBUs will co-operate, for example, by not objecting to saving up cash or withdrawing certain products. This is essential in order to achieve the objective of obtaining a balanced portfolio. While it is true that the technique itself makes no claim to address such problems, there is a danger that management may overlook these problems of application.

Summary

In this first of two chapters concerned with alternative marketing objectives and strategies, we have looked at a range of possible strategic objectives which the marketer may pursue and the alternative broad directions which the marketer may delineate and select from in order to achieve these objectives. Because of the range of possible alternatives available, we have used three relatively simple, but what have proved to be robust and therefore useful, frameworks for identifying alternative marketing objectives and strategies. These are the product life cycle concept, Ansoff's product market scope matrix, and the BCG's product portfolio matrix. These three frameworks can be used to identify the range of strategic options available. They are not mutually exclusive, nor are they the only frameworks available. Used with judgement and discretion, however, they are useful in the development of marketing strategies.

Chapter 10
Marketing Strategies (2)

INTRODUCTION

In the previous chapter we explored the range of possible strategic objectives which the marketer may pursue and the alternative broad directions from which the marketer may select in order to achieve these. In this chapter we look at the alternative strategies for developing a sustainable competitive advantage in order to achieve the objectives established earlier. Again, one of the major difficulties in this area of marketing planning is the enormous range of possible alternatives which are available to a company. Numerous taxonomies of strategic choices are available. As in the previous chapter, we have deliberately limited the scope of our discussion to the range of strategic alternatives which we feel are particularly robust, relevant and therefore useful to the practising marketing manager. In fact, the framework of strategic alternatives used here is essentially along the lines of that developed by the American Michael Porter with his concept of 'generic strategies'. We shall explain this concept shortly, but first we need to establish the meaning and importance of developing a sustainable competitive advantage (SCA).

DEVELOPING A SUSTAINABLE COMPETITIVE ADVANTAGE (SCA)

As we are all aware, today's marketing environment is characterised by intense and aggressive competition. We have already highlighted the importance of analysing competition in Chapter 4 (page 46), but ultimately these analyses of competitors and indeed ultimately the test of the effectiveness of a company's marketing efforts and plans overall is the extent to which the company is able to develop a sustainable competitive advantage. The notion of competitive advantage is something that most marketing managers are familiar with. Put simply, competitive advantage is achieved where a company can offer the market something which is viewed as better than the competition can offer. As we shall see shortly, the basis for being 'better' can be based on various factors. For example, a company might offer 'better' prices, 'better' quality or a 'better' after-sales service. Some studies have identified as many as 80 or more possible ways in which a business can strive to be better than its competitors. However, these studies also indicate that on average most companies concentrate on being better in a few selected areas. Without a competitive advantage, customers have no basis on which to choose between supplier offerings, and hence the organisation is left to the vagaries of the market and random choice. On the other hand, a competitive advantage gives a customer a reason to choose a company's product offering over and above the competition and in this way helps to secure the success of the business. Later, we shall consider the broad alternative generic routes which a company can use to attempt to build a competitive advantage, together with their relative advantages, disadvantages and requirements. But it is not enough for planners that a company should develop merely a transitory edge over its competitors. The competitive advantage needs to be one which can be maintained by the company in the face of what we have already stated to be intense competition – hence the notion of a 'sustainable' competitive advantage. Regardless of the bases used to develop a competitive edge in order for this edge to be an effective SCA, a number of important conditions must be met as follows:

In the face of intense competition in today's marketplace, the company must have a clear idea of how it will develop and maintain a sustainable competitive advantage.

❑ *The SCA must be based on company strengths/marketing assets.* Remember that strategies should reflect what a company is good at and not its weaknesses. Clearly, it does not make sense to try to develop a sustainable competitive advantage using a basis which requires skills and resources which the company simply does not possess.

❑ *The SCA must be based on an assessment of competitor strengths and weaknesses.* In addition to the SCA being based on the organisation's strengths, we must also be careful not to select an approach to developing an SCA where our competitors are even stronger.

❑ *The SCA must be based on customer needs – that is, it must be 'valued' by customers.* Clearly, it does not make sense to attempt to build an SCA around bases which the customer does not consider important in choosing between competitive offerings. Although this sounds obvious, companies do still exhibit 'marketing myopia' in their approach to marketing strategies.

❑ *The SCA must be substantial enough to make a difference.* Relatively marginal differences in competitive advantage are rarely successful in building a sustainable advantage. Ideally, what we are seeking is a competitive advantage of a substantial nature. If nothing else, the competitive advantage needs to be substantial enough for the customer to notice and appreciate the difference.

❑ *The SCA must be sustainable.* As already mentioned, and indeed as highlighted in the term SCA itself, it is vital that the basis chosen for developing a competitive advantage should be one which the company can defend over time. As we shall see, the choice of an SCA strategy is central to the complete range of activities and strategies which a company pursues. The choice of an SCA therefore involves a company in major investment choices and requires a long-term commitment. Put another way, the basis for an SCA and the strategies required to support and implement it is not something which can or should be changed overnight. Clearly, both the environment and markets change over time. Similarly, a successful strategy is always something that competitors will try to attack and/or emulate. It is not being suggested, therefore, that the basis for an SCA must never change; indeed, effective strategies must be flexible and reflect any major changes which threaten the competitiveness of the organisation. However, notwithstanding this, the basis of the SCA is not something which should be changed lightly and should be sustainable for as long as possible over time against the vagaries of the environment and competition.

❑ *The SCA must be translated into each key element of the marketing plan in a consistent manner*. The importance of deciding the basis for an SCA is that virtually every key element of marketing strategy and planning is effectively determined by this decision. For example, market segmentation, targeting and positioning are underpinned by the SCA basis selected. Similarly, the marketing mix must reflect the SCA basis. Having selected how it is to compete in its markets, there should be no inconsistencies in the application of this basis in the marketing plan.

Having discussed the meaning and importance of developing a sustainable competitive advantage and the conditions which an effective SCA must fulfil, we can now turn our attention to the broad alternative strategies which can be used as bases for an SCA.

GENERIC COMPETITIVE STRATEGIES

As already mentioned, research has indicated literally dozens of specific ways in which a business can strive to be better than its competitors, even if companies concentrate on using only a few of these. However, most of this wide variety of ways in which a company can compete may be subsumed under one of three generic competitive strategies. We shall therefore outline and discuss the meaning of the notion of generic strategies which has become so widely accepted and used in strategic marketing planning. We shall then explain the nature of each of the three generic strategies which are available, together with some of the key considerations in choosing between and applying each of them.

   The word 'generic' is defined as 'pertaining to a class of related things'. In the context of strategic marketing planning, this means that we can distinguish between alternative classes of strategic options for developing a sustainable competitive advantage. Each of these alternatives constitutes a generic strategy which the marketer may pursue in an attempt to build an SCA. As already mentioned, it is now generally accepted that there are three such generic strategic alternatives on which to base a competitive advantage. Each of these represents a very different strategic thrust on the part of the organisation. These three major alternative strategies are as follows:

1. Cost leadership.
2. Differentiation.
3. Market segment focus.

Cost leadership

This first generic strategy is based, as the term implies, on developing a competitive advantage around the company which has the 'lowest costs' compared to its competitors in the industry. Clearly, such a strategy suggests that only one company in the industry can achieve a sustainable competitive advantage in this way. Through the achievement of low costs, it is intended that the company will achieve high levels of profit; indeed, all things being equal, the cost leader should be the most profitable company in the market. It is important to stress that pursuing a cost leadership strategy does not mean that the company is competing through lower prices. Rather, the idea is that the cost leader will charge industry average prices but obviously, with lower costs, will enjoy higher profits. This is a feature of cost leadership strategy which is often misunderstood by some marketers. Obviously, given this notion of charging the same or similar prices to an organisation's competition, a cost leadership strategy can only be effective where the cost leader's products or services are perceived by customers as being on a par with its competitors' offerings. Similarly, a cost leadership strategy is only really effective in markets where there is little or no differentiation between competitors' offerings. It is only suitable, therefore, for some markets. This criterion for considering a cost leadership strategy points to some of the risks associated with this generic strategy. For example, where the pursuit of cost leadership leads to, say, lower quality or poorer services to customers, there is a distinct danger that the cost leader will quickly lose the market share. Similarly, where competitors can differentiate their offerings from the cost leader and convince customers of the value of this differentiated offering, the cost leader is left in a vulnerable position.

Although the cost leader can charge industry average prices, it enjoys higher profits by achieving lower costs.

Attempts to achieve cost leadership can be done in the following ways:

❑ A company may secure access to cheaper sources of supply – for example, raw materials, components, and so on.

❑ A company may invest in new manufacturing plant or processes in order to reduce costs.

❑ A company may seek to achieve economies of scale through take-overs and mergers.

❑ A company may seek cost advantages through linkages between different elements of the company's own and supplier value chains.

❑ Cost leadership can be achieved by being the first to market and/ or patent activities.

❑ Cost leadership can be achieved through the effective integration and synergy between different parts of the business.

As already hinted at, there is a danger that the pursuit of cost leadership will lead to a tendency to ignore the needs of customers and the activities of competitors. In other words, it tends to be an inward-looking strategy rather than a customer-oriented one. Clearly, it is also based on being able to maintain a cost advantage over the long-run compared to competitors.

Differentiation

This approach to developing a sustainable competitive advantage is at the other extreme to a cost leadership strategy. Differentiation is based on attempting to create something which is different and unique compared to competition, and which at the same time is valued by customers. The idea of differentiation is that by building in uniqueness to a company's product or service offerings, the company will be able to secure either higher prices and/or a greater market share.

Differentiation can be achieved in the following ways:

❑ Through innovative and distinctive designs – for example, Bang and Olufson.

❑ Through quality engineering, etc – for example, Mercedes.

❑ Through brand and/or corporate imagery – for example, Coca-Cola, IBM.

❑ Through innovative and distinctive distribution channels – for example, Avon.

❑ Through differentiated prices – either higher or lower than competitors.

It is important to stress that the basis for the differentiation strategy must be one which is valued by customers. In addition, the basis ideally must be defendable from competitors. The risks of differentiation are essentially that competitors will imitate the strategy, thereby removing the basis for customer choice. It is also important to recognise that differentiation can be expensive – again, it is important to compare the potential costs of such differentiation with the value placed on it by the marketplace.

Market segment focus

In one sense this is not a completely different generic strategy from either cost leadership or differentiation, as it involves the pursuit of either a cost leadership strategy or a differentiation strategy in selected parts of the market. In other words, it is based on the application of cost leadership or differentiation in a particular segment. However, by far the most effective use of a market segment focus strategy is the one which is based on differentiation rather than on cost leadership. This is because a company which focuses on a small segment of the market can begin to differentiate itself more easily from its competitors because of this specialisation. Indeed, the focused specialisation itself is the source of differentiation.

Small companies in particular can achieve a competitive advantage by focusing on a segment of the market and differentiating themselves from their competitors.

In recent years, many companies have been very successful with this approach to developing a competitive advantage. It may also be called 'niche marketing' and is a particularly successful strategy for smaller companies which are unable to compete on a wider basis in markets against much larger companies.

The main danger of the market segment focus as a generic strategy is that it leaves a company very vulnerable to changes in the market segments on which they have focused. For example, if customer tastes change and the product therefore becomes unfashionable in the target market segment, this can leave a company with nowhere to go. Similarly, larger competitors often attack smaller companies which have developed successful market niches for themselves.

Choosing between generic strategies

Clearly, many factors will affect the choice between these alternative strategies for developing a sustainable competitive advantage – for example, company size and resources, competitor strategies and resources, company objectives, and segment size and attractiveness are important considerations. It is suggested, however, that it is dangerous to try to pursue more than one strategy at the same time. For example, it is impossible to pursue both a cost leadership strategy while at the same time trying to differentiate one's products and services as a basis for competitive advantage. A company which attempts to pursue both strategies runs the risk of being 'stuck in the middle' – that is, achieving successfully neither one nor the other.

Summary

In this chapter we have looked at the alternative strategies for developing a sustainable competitive advantage. In doing so, we have used the notion of generic strategies and specifically the alternatives of cost leadership, differentiation and market segment focus. Each of these strategies has its own requirements and its own relative advantages and disadvantages. The marketer must identify clearly which are the most appropriate to the particular circumstances of the organisation and, having selected the generic strategy, should attempt to pursue this strategy on all fronts.

Chapter 11
Marketing Information Systems

INTRODUCTION

In this chapter we will look at the importance, components and uses of marketing information in the development of the strategic marketing plan.

Modern managers relate to information like a fish relates to water. Increasingly, survival rests on their capacity to obtain and employ it to best advantage, and this is especially true of strategic marketing planning, which now occupies the centre stage in the increasingly volatile and dynamic commercial environment of the late 20th century. Since every manager exists in a different landscape of opportunities and problems, how this information is to be employed presents very particular problems.

There are three broad categories of managerial activity:

❑ Operational control.
❑ Management control.
❑ Strategic planning.

These can be seen as a continuum, with different information needs for each. The same data, however, may be used by different managers in slightly different ways, with each one concentrating on a slightly different aspect. Planners may want less detail in recurrent information than operational controllers, for example.

It is important to differentiate decision analysis, which starts by defining the key decisions for which the manager is responsible and then developing an analytical model for each separate decision to identify the information requirements, and data analysis, which measures the information currently received by the manager and the information needed but not currently received.

Successful marketing invariably rests on good information, and information processing and dissemination are core activities in marketing management. Bringing together the information needs of marketing personnel and the range of information available inside and outside the organisation, lies at the heart of consistent, effective marketing actions in the model organisation. Information needs are, of course, often related to marketing mix variables, and some, such as decisions related to stock levels, are much easier to define and fulfil than others. In volatile and unstable modern markets, however, management decisions are often complex, dealing with unpredictable and dynamic systems. Information needs, on the other hand, are extremely diverse. This range and diversity underlines the need for a systematic approach to gathering, analysing and disseminating information. Some of the typical elements of the marketing information system, which illustrates the diversity and range of information required, are shown in Figure 11.1.

WHY DO WE NEED MARKETING INFORMATION SYSTEMS (MkIS)?

Increased complexity in business requires more data to achieve better performance. Product life cycles have shortened as a consequence of increased competition. This increases information needs as a way of minimising risk and improving the effectiveness and profitability of managerial decision-making. The ubiquity of the marketing concept and the consequent increase in the importance of the marketing manager means that these managers have far greater and more diverse information needs if their effectiveness is to be increased. Many companies have increased in size, and information systems can serve to offset the dispersion and consequent dissipation of available information. Speedy decision-making has become ever more important as the pace and intensity of competition increases. Information and communications technology has made it possible to

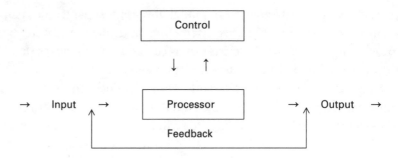

Invoice	Sales	Profitability
Price	By product	By product
Quantity purchased	By product line	By product line
Customer name	By customer class	By customer class
Customer location	By cost centre	By salesperson
Credit terms	By region	
Method of delivery	By salesperson	*Life-cycle analysis*
Date of order	By competitors	Introduction phase
		Growth phase
Annual reports	*Market share*	Maturity phase
Of customers	Inventory	Decline phase
Of competitors	Forecasts	
Of suppliers	Technical service	
Trade association data		
Payroll	*Marketing personnel*	
Departmental budgets	Turnover ratio	
Manufacturing cost	Hiring ratio	
Reports	Transfers	
Accounts receivable	Promotions	
Accounts payable	Absenteeism	
Inventory reports		
Trade journals	*Financial*	
Sales call reports	Credit	
Manning tables	Discount analysis (by	
Personnel department	customer, region, etc)	
reports	Promotional allowances	
Census data	Budgets	
Marketing cost reports	Customer list	
	New accounts	
Market research input		
Audit and panel data		
Special projects		
Customer demand		
schedules		
Questionnaire replies		

Figure 11.1   Typical elements of the marketing information system

record, store and access previously unimaginable amounts of information. The ubiquity of computing and communications technologies has also made it possible for a far wider range of (non-specialist) people to take advantage of these information sources. Marketing information systems (MkIS) are becoming more and more widespread, but they have both positive and negative features. The advantages include speedier and more efficient use of information; thus, performance benefits from the integration of diverse and dispersed information within large organisations. A second advantage is the fuller exploitation of the marketing concept and the tailoring of information retrieved to the specific needs of an individual. A third advantage is the speedier identification of new trends and the more effective use of information gathered for other purposes – for example, sales data. We can also achieve a closer control over the marketing plan by means of performance indicators which makes it more difficult to hide, ignore or suppress information which may be damaging or inconvenient – for example, bad sales figures or customer feedback.

As mentioned earlier, however, there are also disadvantages. These can be categorised into those which are related to the organisation, and those which are of a general nature. Organisational disadvantages may involve problems caused by faulty integration between subsystems – for example, producing misleading information. The system also requires new job and skill requirements, which some organisations may find problematic. Finally, there have been problems, as with other IT applications, in getting the needs of the users properly incorporated into the systems designed by computer engineers. Often, systems prove difficult to use or cannot accommodate the objectives of the 'lay' user. General problems are diverse. At the moment, some firms would find this kind of system inappropriate and wasteful of resources. Fashion alone is not a good reason to implement such a system. There is a danger of rejecting 'traditional' methods of record-keeping and accounting in favour of computers when these do not offer significant advantages. The rapid and radical changes which these systems may bring can constitute a danger to the firm.

MkIS are a supplement to, rather than a replacement for,

marketing research, which is still needed for specific topics. Computerised data may tend to generate over-confidence because of its polished appearance. The novelty of the system should not be overemphasised – recent developments have made them more widely available, and increased capacities for storage and analysis. The benefits of these systems are unequally distributed, just as the needs of potential users are diverse. This poses particular challenges to the designers of systems to fit the data output to the needs and capacities of the various users. It is important to resist the danger of using the power and flexibility of the computer just because it is there, rather than keep the needs of the user directly in mind – it should be 'need-to-know', rather than 'nice-to-know', data. The quality and salience of the data are important, not the volume. Systems sometimes fail to render data into concise usable forms. Time considerations should always be borne in mind. The danger is that firms will attempt to establish comprehensive 'once-and-for-all' systems in unrealistically short periods of time. Information for its own sake can be counter-productive. Systems should be developed with a firm connection to the practical 'real world' dimensions of the marketing manager's world, resisting the temptation to gather and analyse information for no immediate good reason. When users do not fully understand how a system works, a dangerous reliance can develop, with disastrous results should the system malfunction or (more often) be subject to inappropriate use. The other important need here is for the manager to provide feedback and input which will enable the system to be upgraded when necessary, to accommodate the inevitable changes which occur in business environments and systems.

Use your discrimination when storing information on the computer: relevance and quality take priority over volume.

MANAGEMENT INFORMATION NEEDS

Some experts divide managerial activities into three categories: operational control, management control and strategic planning – each of which may be subdivided, with distinctive informational needs related to each role within the organisation. It is possible to conceive of these categories as a continuum, with different attributes of the same information being relevant to different activities along that continuum. Thus, planners will not need great detail in non-recurrent external information, and operational controllers will concentrate on regular supplies of internal information, with precise details on clearly specified areas.

It is useful to distinguish between decision analysis in modern management practice and traditional data analysis. The latter measures the information currently received by the manager, and also defines that information which the manager needs but does not receive. Decision analysis begins by defining the key decisions for which a manager holds responsibility and proceeds to develop an analytical model for separate decisions, in order to arrive at a definition of information requirements. Since good information is so important for successful marketing, we could argue that marketing management is first and foremost concerned with information processing, and that the primary function of any MkIS is to achieve the most effective use of internal and external information in order to satisfy the identified information needs of decision-makers within the organisation.

Some information needs to be relatively easily specified – for example, practical issues such as control over stock levels – and this type of information can be dealt with by traditional data analysis. Many managers, however, are working with highly unpredictable, dynamic and non-recurrent problems, and here, formal information systems may well not be able to supply the information which is needed. It is often difficult for managers to anticipate their information needs and, as a consequence, the design of systems to satisfy these needs is a constant challenge, and perhaps one which is always in need of change and review.

Because information systems are not always the answer to supplying the required information, the design of systems needs to be under constant review.

INFORMATION SYSTEMS AND SYSTEMS THEORY

Systems theory has been attractive to marketing managers because it emphasises the diversity of the parts in the system and the dynamic nature of the process of which it is a part. This stresses the importance of interaction and integration in the decision process, rather than emphasising a static, particularistic approach. It also allows the decision-makers to organise thinking about a particular process by providing a framework, to perceive connections between elements within that situation, and to produce a structure for analysis planning and control. A number of different types of system may be included under the rubric of information systems. These include electronic data processing (EDP) which involves basic data processing, with no common data base. This may be improved by integrating data processing and establishing a common data base. This may be said to be slightly less sophisticated than a true management information system (MIS). Decision support systems (DSS) involve an integrated information system made up of the decision-maker, decision models and a data base, in order to support decisions. This can be used, for example, for planning management information systems. It is, at the most basic level, a system which provides each decision-maker within the organisation with the information needed to arrive at decisions, and to develop plans and establish controls in areas of responsibility. The modern view is that, as management information systems become increasingly sophisticated, it makes more sense to talk of decision support systems.

The marketing information system is a subsystem of broader management information or decision support systems. It aims to provide management with information about the present and future state of its markets and also market responses to company and/or competitor actions. Some see it as a carefully designed set of methods and procedures by means of which information which is relevant to particular managers is made available in an orderly way. MkIS is generally agreed to be a highly structured interacting mixture of people, machines and organisational procedures, involving elements and material from inside and outside the organisation. The perception of information systems as synonymous with market research is less common today, as the range of information, providers and forms of analysis grow, owing to the ubiquity of systems involving the recording, storage, retrieval and analysis of commercially salient information. Most marketers would now see MkIS as an important aid to marketing management decisions, but recognise that other systems are also important – for example, marketing intelligence, accounting information, marketing research proper, and also systems for modelling and analysing managerial problems. MkIS involve many different applications. These include:

❏ Data storage and retrieval.
❏ Monitoring systems.
❏ Analytical information systems providing 'what if?' analysis.
❏ Current awareness subsystems using databases.
❏ 'In depth and crisis information' subsystems using marketing research techniques.
❏ 'Incidental information' subsystems using marketing intelligence.

Distinctions between market research and marketing information systems

Market research information and activity are subactivities within the overall system of marketing information, but provide only part of the information which would be used in a marketing information system. MkIS involves a much wider range of information, which may have many mundane or routine uses, contrasting with the high cost, high quality, direct relevance and high degree of significance of marketing research findings, particularly in the case of primary research material.

CONSTITUENT ELEMENTS IN MARKETING INFORMATION SYSTEMS

MkIS can be applied at every level within the company from micro to macro. The elements of a marketing information system are generally accepted to comprise the following:

❏ *The internal accounting system* uses data which the firm gathers in order to carry out accounting functions.
❏ *Marketing intelligence* includes the collection of data about the market which will be available to the firm through contacts with customers, direct experience of business operations, reports prepared by salesmen and other personnel. It is usually in an unstructured and unquantified form, but may nevertheless be highly useful.
❏ *Marketing Research* involves information which is gathered and analysed to address market-related problems which are specific to the company involved.

❏ *Marketing decision support system* comprises the application of various scientific or statistical methods and modes of analysis to management problems. Other versions would distinguish between the model bank and the information bank, the former storing data which has been reduced into a usable form, while the latter consists of behavioural, analytical and planning models.

DESIGN OF THE SYSTEMS

It is essential to design the marketing information system to support the decision-maker's information needs if it is to be effective.

Clearly, if MkIS are to be adopted successfully, it is essential that the design of the system should be logical, thorough and adequate to the particular needs of the organisation involved. Although structures may well vary according to these specific needs, the following general framework has been proposed. This is shown in Figure 11.2 below:

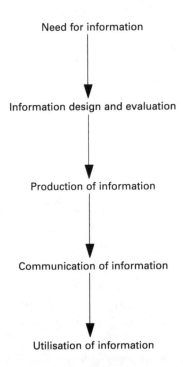

Figure 11.2   A basic framework for designing the marketing information system

This framework for the planning process will provide the basis on which the specific conformation of the individual information system may be based.

ORGANISATIONAL RESPONSES TO INFORMATION SYSTEMS

Marketing information systems are bound to have an impact on the functioning of an organisation, and some remedial responses may be necessary. These range from the 'clean piece of paper' approach, in which the organisation is restructured from top to bottom; the 'committee' approach, in which resources and expertise which are necessary for the introduction of MkIS are pooled; the 'low level' approach, in which the introduction of the system is assigned to a junior manager; the 'information co-ordinator' approach, in which responsibility is assigned to a single manager who is able to operate across system areas, leaving the original organisational structure virtually intact.

SUCCESSES AND FAILURES OF MkIS

The initial adoption of MkIS has proved patchy, and the first firms to use the systems tended to stick to a limited and unsophisticated range of issues and applications. Researchers found that many firms which resisted the introduction of such systems often 'saw no real use' of them or else felt that staff lacked the knowledge or motivation to make good use of them. Many small companies, in the initial period, felt that the investment involved was out of proportion to the benefits which could be derived, or they believed that the nature of their business operations – being diverse, for example or highly decen-tralised – was likely to make an MkIS unworkable or irrelevant. This has changed. The main reasons why systems are now being adopted relate to the gradual evolution of these systems as part of an overall marketing function as a decision aid – in a sense, marketing managers have 'grown into' them – while the explosion of IT resources, experience and skill has had a huge impact. Many of the skills which are necessary to use such systems are now basic to management

The gradual adoption of marketing information systems has been a revolutionary process, making information more readily available and transforming management structures.

practice. The 'novelty' factor has now all but disappeared, and managers are coming to recognise the power and essential strategic value of information in the marketing processes. Some experts have argued, for example, that the open availability of information is transforming management structures as the old hierarchies, based on the control of information, are being delayered, with many levels of middle management no longer having a *raison d'être*. Others have compared the redistribution of power which is involved, to the changing position of the Christian Church when its monopoly over the knowledge of the Bible was overturned by the invention of the printing press, making the word of God directly available to ordinary people. Everyone is agreed that a revolution is underway, and that information is transforming the way in which business activity takes place. Marketing is at the heart of this change.

Summary

In this chapter we have examined the importance, components and potential uses of the marketing information system. Information is the lifeblood of marketing decisions and should be used throughout the design, implementation and control of strategic marketing plans. In order to be effective, it is essential to design the system with a view to supporting the decision-makers' information needs.

Chapter 12

The Marketing Mix Plan

INTRODUCTION

In this chapter we will move from the analysis stages of the strategic marketing plan through to the consideration of action programmes which are designed to achieve overall marketing objectives and positioning strategies in selected target markets. We shall do this by examining the elements of what has come to be termed 'the marketing mix'.

THE ROLE OF THE MARKETING MIX IN SATISFYING CUSTOMER NEEDS

The activity of marketing involves making decisions and setting policies in key areas which will meet precisely identified consumer needs. A product is rarely, if ever, just a physical entity. Any product can be seen as the outcome of decisions which relate not only to its form, composition, appearance, and so on, but also to the qualities or characteristics which buyers and users perceive it to have – the image, performance, status, value, and so on, which they believe it represents.

These perceptions are founded on the qualities which have attributed to the product and how it is evaluated in relation to competitors and substitutes, on the basis not only of its objective characteristics (appearance, weight, size, colour, smell, and so on) but also of less tangible aspects, such as the meaning or symbolic value which is given to product characteristics – for example, the vintage or place of origin of food or wine, or the maker's label for a garment. Consumer perceptions create value which is added to the product and contributes extra satisfaction to the consumer.

It follows that the overall process of marketing is then crucial to the way in which the product is perceived by consumers and the satisfactions which the consumer ultimately derives from the product. In order to arrive at the most effective combination of factors in the process of marketing to create a product which is significantly superior to its competitors in providing satisfactions to consumer needs involves developing the marketing mix, since different dimensions of the marketing process can add value in different ways. This has been conceived in a number of different ways, but the most famous expression of the idea of the marketing mix involves the 'four Ps' – product, place, price and promotion. More recently, however, these original four elements of the marketing mix have been extended to take account of the growth and importance of services marketing in economies.

WHAT IS THE MARKETING MIX?

The marketing mix is the set of controllable variables which the manager modifies in order to achieve particular objectives within the marketing plan. Typically, these relate to the attempt to satisfy the needs of the target market, to implement predetermined positioning strategies in these target markets, and to achieve other organisational objectives.

The decision areas which are involved may be described in a number of ways. As already mentioned, however, the classic notion of the elements of the marketing mix were based on product, price, promotion and place. These elements comprise the tactics of the detailed methods and techniques to be employed in implementing marketing strategies. They are best described as the 'nuts and bolts' of the marketing operation and involve decisions regarding the detailed activities to be undertaken in the marketing plan. Because of this, the marketing mix encompasses a myriad of possible decisions and action plans. An indication of some of the key decision areas encompassed by each element of the 'four Ps' of the marketing mix are shown below.

Product

Overall, product decisions concern strategies which relate to what is being offered to customers. It involves decisions such as: What is to be our product range? What will be the balance between the different products in the range? What is to be the product mix and depth? Product decisions include issues such as: Which products should we actually offer? How should we aim to position these products within the market?

As part of product decisions, it will be necessary to review the following considerations:

❑ The different aspects of style.
❑ What features the product(s) need to offer.
❑ What quality will be appropriate in terms of the target consumer and the strategic objectives of the company.
❑ How the product should be branded and what issues are involved.
❑ What kind of packaging is needed and what functions it needs to accomplish.

It is now generally recognised, however, that the 'product' involves more than just the physical product and even its branding and packaging. In addition to this core level of the product, we also need to consider additional attributes which can be offered to customers alongside the core product which may give us a competitive edge. These additional attributes are often referred to as the augmented product.

Elements of the augmented product offering include the following:

❑ What terms do we need to offer when the product is being sold (for instance, special credit arrangements)?
❑ Do we need to provide special service dimensions (for instance, special guarantees, advice on usage or problem solving, or arrangements to maintain or repair the product)?

It is now suggested that these augmented product elements are among the most important in customer choice and in securing a competitive advantage.

One of the most important areas of product management is the management of new and modified products. Most marketers are now familiar with the concept of the product life cycle which suggests that products pass through different stages during their lives but, more importantly, in the context of new product management, also suggests that products and brands have finite lives. Eventually, even the most successful products and brands will begin to experience falling sales and diminishing profits. Because of this, it is vital that the marketing manager should be alert to the need to introduce either improved or new products in order to maintain sales and profits. Although much criticised as a planning tool for marketers, there is no doubt that this underpinning notion of finite lives in the product life cycle concept is sound and therefore new product management is an essential part of managing the product element of the marketing mix. The following represent some of the decisions which marketing managers have to make regarding managing products over their life cycle and the introduction of new ones:

The maintenance of sales and profits depends on an awareness of a product's life cycle and knowing when to modify or withdraw it, or when to replace it with a new product.

❑ Which products need to be withdrawn.
❑ Which products need to be modified.
❑ Which products need to be phased out.
❑ Which products need to be introduced.

New product development and management is among the most risky and difficult areas for the organisation. An effective process for developing and launching new products involves the following steps.

Idea generation

The first stage of new product development involves generating new product concepts and ideas. Some companies use creativity techniques to generate new product ideas, but one of the best sources for successful new product ideas comes from the market itself, and in particular from researching the unmet needs of customers.

Screening

The second stage of new product development involves a preliminary assessment of the new product ideas which were generated earlier. A screening system should enable the marketer to gauge if the product idea has sufficient merit to warrant further investigation and the development of prototypes, marketing testing, and so on. Overall, the screening process should assess if the idea is compatible with customer and market needs, and with company resources.

Business analysis

If a product passes the preliminary screening stage, then a more detailed investigation of the market and financial potential of the product can be undertaken. This may involve assessing factors such as overall market size, competitor products (if any), likely levels of investment and possible rates of return.

Product development and market testing

If business analysis suggest a profitable opportunity for the new product, we may now proceed to the stage of developing the product so that market testing can be undertaken. Market testing may involve concept testing, particularly through the use of focus groups, which comprise small group interviews with potential target customers, and/or test marketing where the product is launched in a test area on a limited scale to assess potential customer response.

Commercialisation and launch

If market testing proves successful, the new product may then be taken to the stage of commercialisation and launch. At this stage, detailed product decisions concerning, for example, packaging will be finalised; promotional and other material will be produced; dealers will be recruited and briefed; and the salesforce will be trained. Marketers have identified that in many markets a small group of people constitutes the target market for a new product launch. This group is often referred to as the innovator group. Innovators are those people in a market who are the first to try and adopt new products, and therefore they constitute an important target market when new products are launched. Marketers are now able to identify these innovators in markets and can therefore address their marketing to them.

Price

Price decisions need to relate to a number of different areas. For instance, in the case of the launch of new products, strategic objectives such as establishing a market share may involve minimal profit or even, in some cases, below-cost pricing; the same cost-cutting strategy may be pursued as a way of establishing market dominance. Price decisions may also involve considering the way in which products are perceived – if we want to position a product in the 'prestige' sector of a market, then prices need to be appropriate, low prices are usually associated with inferior quality or lack of a status cachet. The most important consideration in reaching the pricing decision, however, is the price charged by competitors. Arriving at a price without reference to what others are offering by beginning, for example, with the costs of manufacture, and so on, and then adding on a 'margin' (which is called 'cost-plus' pricing) is a very dangerous pursuit indeed, and may only be usable in a very few situations.

The price charged by competitors is the most important factor in reaching the pricing decision.

Pricing decisions include, for example, decisions regarding the following:

❏ Price levels.
❏ Price changes.
❏ Discounts.
❏ Credit terms.
❏ Allowances.

Promotion

Promotion involves communicating various kinds of messages to those who may be involved, directly or indirectly, in the activities surrounding the consumption of products or services which the company has for sale. It involves typically a number of different sorts of activities, apart from advertising which most people think of when this aspect of marketing is mentioned. Two types of activity are recognised by marketers themselves. Below-the-line activities are those which involve getting the message across through media and channels which do not involve paying a commission (the 'line' referred to derives from the balance sheet on which costs and profits are recorded and calculated). Above-the-line activities – which include paid advertising – do involve the payment of a commission.

Although many promotional messages involve attempts to persuade consumers to purchase, many different objectives may also be pursued – for instance, providing information about how to use a product or trying to communicate the characteristics of the product's personality so that consumers will identify with the satisfactions that the product is intended to provide when it is used.

Many different types of promotional tools are available to the marketer. As already mentioned, most non-marketing specialists think only of advertising when they consider marketing promotion. However, there are literally dozens of marketing communications tools. It is conventional in marketing circles to refer to the 'marketing communications mix' when describing these different tools. The main elements of this mix are:

❑ Advertising.
❑ Sales promotion.
❑ Personal selling.
❑ Publicity and public relations.

Conventionally, direct marketing communications and sponsorship were considered as part of the general heading of sales promotion, but they are now of such importance in terms of their widespread use that these two marketing communications tools are often considered in addition to the four main elements listed above. Within each of these main elements of the communications mix there is a large number of individual communications/promotional vehicles. For example, sales promotion includes free offers, competitions, merchandising deals, self-liquidating offers and so on.

In planning the marketing communications mix, clearly decisions must be made regarding not only the overall budget for marketing communications but also how this is to be allocated between the different elements of the mix. Many factors affect the decision regarding allocation, including, for example, the type of product market, company resources, customer targets, and so on.

Place, or Channels of Distribution

The place where a product is offered for sale will have important implications for the way in which consumers perceive the merchandise. The image of the store in which a product is bought does affect the way in which consumers, or 'prospects', perceive their

Customers' perceptions of a product are influenced by the store where they purchased it, so retail outlets should be chosen with care.

purchase. Those seeking to develop a particular brand image will seek to place their products on the shelves of the appropriate retailer. If we are seeking to mass market a product, for instance, it will be counter-productive to place it on the shelves of an élite, exclusive retailer. Similarly, those aiming to communicate a message of high-quality exclusivity need to keep their products off the shelves of the 'pile-em-high-and-sell-em-cheap' brigade.

Other issues of availability relate to consumer perceptions of service – having an automobile readily available in precisely the colour which the customer requests conveys an important message to the customer about the efficiency and service-orientation of the company concerned. New systems of distribution, pioneered by the Japanese and called JIT (just-in-time) systems, enable customer service to be achieved without the necessity of holding extensive, and expensive, stocks of products, such as automobiles. In this case, individual cars are made to the requirements of the customer and delivered to the retailer within a few days. Other systems, such as computer stock inventories, allow chains of retailers to meet customer needs by calling on stocks held nationally rather than in an individual store.

Some of the decisions which affect the placement of a product are as follows:

❑ Channel coverage – for example, intensive versus selective.
❑ Channel levels – for example, direct versus indirect channels.
❑ Types of intermediaries to be used.
❑ Terms and responsibilities of channel members.
❑ Delivery and ordering schedules and conditions.
❑ Warehousing, storage and stocking.
❑ Back-up services with regard to delivery systems.

These, then, are the original core elements of the marketing mix. As mentioned earlier, however, the growth of services marketing has given rise to the addition of a further three elements to the original four elements of the mix. These are as follows:

People

Services marketing involves a high 'people content' element. For example, when choosing a hairdresser, a restaurant or even a dentist, customers are heavily swayed by their perceptions of the person(s) providing the service. A major reason for this is, of course, that the provider is often in direct contact with the customer. Services marketers must pay particular attention, therefore, to the training and skills of their employees as these constitute a key part of their marketing mix.

Physical Evidence

Many service products are essentially intangible. What this means is that it is difficult or impossible for the customer to assess, for example, the quality of the service prior to its consumption. Thus, a management consultant's product which is comprised mainly of his or her 'professional expertise', is essentially intangible. Because of this, the marketer must plan carefully the nature of the service offering by managing its physical evidence, such as, for example, the facilities, equipment, and so on.

Process

Again related to both the people content and the intangibility aspects of service products, the final element of the contemporary marketing mix relates to how the service is provided to customers. For example, procedures for dealing with customers at the point of sale and the supply of the service itself are an important element of marketing a service. The marketer must design such systems, including the training of personnel who have contact with customers, so that the desired level of quality of service supply is maintained in all customer contacts.

FACTORS AFFECTING MARKETING MIX DECISIONS

Clearly, decisions about the marketing mix are wide-ranging and potentially complex. Many factors affect the choice of what will constitute an effective and appropriate marketing mix, some of which we have discussed already, but among the most important factors which will shape marketing mix decisions are the following:

❏ Overall corporate and marketing objectives.
❏ Target markets and customers.
❏ Positioning strategies.
❏ Competitor strategies.
❏ Organisational resources.

Summary

In this chapter we have looked at the tools which are available to the marketer for implementing detailed marketing programmes. These tools, which originally comprised the elements of product, price, place and promotion, we have referred to as the marketing mix. Each of these elements, however, is in turn comprised of a number of subelements or decision areas which the marketer must plan. More recently, the growth of service product markets has given rise to a further three elements in the marketing mix – namely, people, physical evidence and process. The marketing mix must reflect a number of key considerations, in particular target market customers and positioning strategies. Above all, the elements of the mix must be designed to be consistent, one with another and with the overall corporate and marketing strategies.

Chapter 13
Sales Forecasting

INTRODUCTION

The changing and complex business environment, coupled with the increasing importance of information and decision support systems (see Chapter 11) have meant that the techniques used to forecast markets have become more and more of a central issue for the marketing strategist. Decisions based on guesses and hunches are no longer so easy to live with should they prove to be wrong, and organisations which do not have access to anything other than these primitive 'rule-of-thumb' techniques are likely to find themselves in difficulties, if not struggling for survival.

Planning is at the heart of modern scientific management, and the strategies and tactics which it uses depend on reliable information which can be incorporated into the planning process. In this chapter we will look at the information provided by sales forecasting and how this is used in the planning process.

DEFINING FORECASTING

Before we develop a strategy or a broad plan which aims to achieve a specific goal and have begun to formulate the tactics, the specific methods by which the plan is to be achieved, it is necessary to take into account the framework, the environment and the market conditions within which these plans operate. We need therefore to produce, as accurately as possible, a prediction of those conditions, to try to look into the future and forecast the situation. Such a prediction may include:

❏ The total size of the market.
❏ The sales of different brands.
❏ A breakdown by companies, by products, by types of customer.

Clearly, when planning, it is essential to be able to predict sales for a product in order to be able to gauge what proportion of total sizes might be achieved by the company; what market share might be expected and what might be aimed for as a consequence of adopting particular strategies.

Forecasting sales for the entire market is referred to as 'market forecasting'.

Forecasting sales for a company is referred to as 'sales forecasting'. Such forecasts lie at the heart of strategic marketing planning and evaluation, and the procedures which are used must be as accurate and as reliable as possible since the results will establish the likely success or failure of any plans which might be developed.

A number of key dimensions are involved, the first of these being the time-scale of the forecast.

TIME-SCALES IN FORECASTING

Time-scales can be short, medium or long term. Short-term forecasts are typically used for continuous in-house activities such as production planning (where production staff need to know what the demands are likely to be, as the market fluctuates according to the operation of a host of different factors) and financial accounting (which is concerned with managing resources in order to buy in materials, labour, machinery, and so on, which are needed to produce goods and resources to meet market demands but which also ensures that these resources are co-ordinated to the actual demands within the market).

Medium-term forecasts are needed to manage the company over the budget period ahead, which is usually a one-year period. Business budgets will be based on this forecast and, should it prove incorrect, then there are likely to be penalties for the company. An over-optimistic forecast will produce a company overspend, with the consequence that stockholding, and the consequent non-productive use of capital, will be needlessly high. An excessively pessimistic forecast is likely to result in cash-flow problems and the loss of sales opportunities, since the plan does not allow for sufficient production to meet actual demand or to accommodate unanticipated consumer needs.

The accuracy of the sales forecast is of prime importance for the success of the company's plans.

Long-term sales forecasts are produced as one of the key elements in major strategic decision-making. These can cover periods ranging from 5 years to more than 20 years ahead, according to the horizons of the company concerned. Clearly, for large companies operating nowadays in global markets, such plans are essential – building factories and increasing salesforces involve significant commitments in terms of resources and carry major implications for any organisation. Long-term planning is needed in order to anticipate demand, and to accommodate changes in market size and conditions. In many cases, plans need to be long term because the processes of raising capital, negotiating contracts and carrying out building work are inevitably long-term propositions.

THE DIFFERENT USES OF THE SALES FORECAST

Forecasts aim to predict a company's sales. This information can be accomplished by:

❏ Directly calculating the company's likely sales.
❏ Forecasting the *total* market and then deriving the company's likely share from the predicted total.

Different departments within the organisation need different information from the forecasts which are produced.

Finance departments require forecasting in the medium term so that they can prepare company budgets which cost out company expenditures, income and assets. Capital, of course, needs to be available in the longer term in order to meet expansion requirements, too.

Purchasing departments are more interested in forecasts which are couched in the short to medium time-scale. They must be able to plan purchasing in advance and not simply to respond to specific requisition requests from the production departments, since this allows buyers time to develop more advantageous contacts and contracts, and to use 'lead time' for effective negotiation, rather than having to respond to immediate needs and face the problems which are likely to be involved.

Human Resource Management departments require medium-and long-term forecasts since they need to know, for recruitment purposes, what the manpower and training demands will be as a consequence of market change – how many and what kinds of workers will be needed as a consequence of the size of markets, and the kinds of products and production technologies which are likely to be involved.

Production departments are generally focused on the short term to enable them to plan their manufacturing programmes. These are essentially up to three months in advance, although this can be longer for some types of products. If they can be given advance warning by means of sales forecasts, the more effectively this production can be planned.

Research & Development departments also need forecasts to direct activity into areas which are likely to be profitable for company development. This means that they are most likely to be concerned with long-term forecasts, as well as with information which describes shifts in both market size and distribution, and the likely occurrence of behavioural and attitudinal changes. For example, how are changing behaviours and public attitudes to the environment likely to impact on the way in which we consume?

Marketing is, of course, generally the department which actually carries out the forecast, but in a modern company, marketing departments will play a much more substantial role. In addition to the long-established need for marketing departments to plan and execute sales promotions, advertising campaigns, and so on, marketing departments now are involved centrally in developing strategies which aim to develop or 'grow' markets. Advertising and other forms of promotional activity, as well as the other elements of the marketing mix (see Chapter 12), are crucial to the achievement of the market share and the exploitation of the expanded market potential. For the effective implementation of marketing programmes, the marketing department will be most concerned with medium-term forecasts in order to acquire the appropriate marketing appropriation, and to establish and monitor the execution of marketing strategies. The longer term forecast, however, will also be of crucial concern to strategic marketing. The market structures, such as middlemen and retailing contracts, upon which much successful marketing hinges, may require a great deal of time and effort to develop effectively, and if changes are needed, then this will require significant periods of time to put in train.

Forecasting, then, is needed by all departments within an organisation, and upon the accuracy of the forecast may depend the success or failure of the company's plans. There are a number of different techniques which might be employed to produce forecasts, and we need to consider their debits and merits.

> **Information from the sales forecast will be used in different ways by the various departments in an organisation.**

TECHNIQUES OF FORECASTING

There are two main forms of forecasting technique: *subjective* techniques, also called 'judgemental' methods, which are not primarily based on mathematical or statistical calculations; and *objective* techniques, which are primarily mathematical. We shall now describe these two main forms of forecasting technique in more detail.

Subjective methods of forecasting

Although often considered unreliable and naïve, and able to offer only a rough guide to trends, subjective methods of prediction are widely used and may be appropriate because of the lack of alternatives, the unavailability of the requisite data, or the nature of the issue which is being considered. They can also be an important complement to mathematically based predictions. A number of different techniques might be used, as follows:

❑ *Consumer user surveys*, sometimes referred to as the 'market research method', involves canvassing customers to ask about their purchasing intentions in the forecasting period. This seems intuitively to be a plausible and sensible method, but problems are involved. Customers tend to be over-optimistic or unrealistic about what they intend to do, which gives a misleading impression of what is likely to happen in reality. In addition, this method usually necessitates obtaining a sample of customers who can represent the likely intentions of a much larger number. This often causes problems since it is relatively easy to select an unrepresentative sample without being able to identify the source of this unrepresentativeness: the consequence is a misleading impression of how the population as a whole is likely to behave.

❑ *Panels of executive/expert opinion* are sometimes called the 'jury method'. Those consulted have insider or expert knowledge about the topic with which the forecast is concerned. A body of such experts is consulted, typically ranging from external personnel such as investment analysts, to employees within the client organisation who have expertise in the requisite areas. Experts usually confer in committees and prepare a report which includes a ready-made forecast which can be defended in committee and modified according to agreements reached with other experts and interested parties.

The findings of this method are obviously useful, but they are based, ultimately, upon the opinions of the participant. In addition, they are expensive in terms of manpower resources, and since this is a 'top down' method, it produces a figure which must subsequently be apportioned over individual products and sales territory, so that it does not suit the need for detail which some forecasts undoubtedly have.

❑ *Sales force composites* by contrast, are 'bottom up' methods whereby each member of the salesforce prepares an individual forecast which relates to the territory for which he or she is responsible. After discussion with the sales manager or area/divisional manager, the sales forecasts are agreed. Thus, a picture of the forecast is built up, area by area, and product by product. For this reason, this method is sometimes called the 'grass roots' approach.

A related technique is referred to as 'detecting differences in figures' whereby the sales manager and field salesforce each prepare forecasts separately, then bring them together to find a compromise. There are bound to be issues concerned with this method, however, when such forecasts are ultimately linked to commissions and rewards, by way of sales quotas or targets, as they often are. This will tend to lead the salespeople involved to produce pessimistic forecasts. Without such a link, conversely, forecasts tend to be optimistic. Such accounts tend to be unreliable because of the limited perspective of those who produce them – personal experience is the sole basis, and few macro-factors are taken into account.

❏ *The Delphi Method* involves choosing participants on a similar basis to the panel of experts approach. The participants of the Delphi Method, however, prepare individual forecasts which are discussed with the project leader in order to discuss the decision criteria which have been used after the forecast has been made. Forecasts are then amended in accordance with the results of this discussion. Although figures may well be produced, such forecasts are directed more towards gathering a general impression or feeling of how a likely market will develop, which often, of course, produces a generalised and qualitative account.

In marketing terms, this approach is unlikely to prove appropriate for the production of detailed, product-by-product forecasts, and is generally more useful for gaining an appreciation of the likely impact of, for example, new technologies.

❏ *The Bayesian Decision Theory* is a mixture of subjectivity and objectivity. It is a mathematically based technique which uses the principle of 'decision trees'. These are network diagrams which are used to represent similar issues to critical path analysis diagrams, which estimate the probabilities of various events over the network.

Subjective techniques, then, are deficient because they do not permit an evaluation of their levels of certainty. The main use of such techniques, and their true value, derives from the fact that they can be produced in the absence of a great deal of concrete data and can employ expertise (from within and without the organisation which is preparing them) which otherwise it would not be able to use.

Subjective techniques are, of course, subject to misuse and misinterpretation. Biases can easily be introduced, and their results must always be interpreted with caution and reservation. They are, however, an essential complement to quantitatively based forecasts, and the insight which they provide enables us to make much more sense of, and to give deeper significance to, the data which quantitative forecasts provide.

Objective methods of forecasting

These are sometimes referred to as 'mathematical techniques', and have become increasingly important as computing has spread the application of sophisticated statistical methods in business decision-making far beyond the previously exclusive realm of the expert. Some of the more widely used objective methods are as follows:

❏ *Trend projection* (of past sales) is a graphical technique in which an aggregated line of previous sales is plotted, and future sales are forecast by extending the plotted line into the future over the forecast period. This is a very simple method, but it faces the acute disadvantage that, since it is based on aggregation, it smooths out the fluctuations in the previous sales line so that it is unable to predict sharp down-or up-turns in actual sales. Neither can it take account of the significance of changes over time in the series which it uses – no differences in 'weight' or significance are given to earlier or later data, so that if recent data shows a strong improvement (because of new management or investment in plant or research), or else reflects a temporary, but untypical down-turn in the long-term performance of the company, then this will give a misleading prediction of likely sales in the forecast period.

❏ *Exponential smoothing* represents an attempt to overcome the limitations of trend projection. This is a mathematical technique which apportions different weightings to earlier or later points of the data in the series. Forecasters may then determine the weightings to be applied in order to modify the results of the projection according to the way in which the data is manipulated, introducing judgement about the significance of different sections of the series.

❏ *Z (or 'Zee') charts* take data from the previous year and graphically represent it, so that the top line is the moving annual total – the previous 12 months cumulative data month by month, obtained by deleting the month 12 months earlier, and adding on the current month. The diagonal line (of the Z-shape) is the cumulative data for the year, and here data is added on cumulatively month by month. The bottom line is month-by-month data, starting at the beginning of the year and finishing at the end. This permits an easy comparison of different brand or product lines, and also enables the swift identification of peaks and troughs in monthly sales.

❑ *Time series analysis* is a graphical method which is useful when seasonality plays a significant part in the marketing of a product. Peaks and troughs which become apparent over time, and in many cases are repeated year by year, are fixed features of these series. Seasonality factors are measured in terms of how much they deviate from the aggregate trend. The latter is then included in the graph and extended into the forecasting period. Seasonal factors are then included in the trend line to produce the forecast.

   Where fluctuations can be accommodated, this kind of research obviously offers a significant advantage over the more direct and simple forms of projecting trends over time, and is especially useful where seasonality is so important.

❑ *Correlation analysis* is a mathematical approach which is concerned with the relationship between two sets of variables, but does not seek to explore the relationship between each of them. In fact, there may be no discernible or direct relation between them, but where there is a mathematical relation, a statistical correlation between measurable changes in their value, this can be used as a means of forecasting.

   More recent developments in this area include leading indicator research and econometric model building. These involve the employment of certain macro-economic indicators (for instance, the rate of growth or changes in the unemployment figures), which are then correlated with, for example, the sales of certain products (say, motor cars or VCRs), and a statistical relationship is derived. Such studies occasionally show that these indicators may precede changes in sales performance by a certain time period. If this relationship can be established reliably over a number of years, it can be used as a predictive indicator.

These indicators are an excellent way of predicting shifts in sales, although the forecaster faces the problem of not under-standing the linkages between these indicators and sales figures. Such correlations are common in economic and social analysis, where they are much debated. In marketing, however, the practical value and reliability of these indicators outweighs the importance of unravelling the underlying behavioural connec-tions.

❏ *Regression analysis* also examines the relationships between vari-ables, but is also concerned with the underlying causal pattern. Consequently, these are sometimes called 'causal methods'. For example, we may be interested in the relationship between the number of refrigerators and the volume of fish fingers being sold. It is by no means obvious which of these 'causes' the other – these relationships may be lagged or leading so that refrigerator sales are 'led' by the consumption of frozen foods, or the increased sales of refrigerators generate increased usage of frozen foods, including fish fingers.

Summary

In this chapter we have looked at the importance and uses of sales forecasting in developing marketing strategies. We have examined the various dimensions of forecasts, including the time-scales which forecasts encompass, and the uses to which the sales forecasts may be put. We have also briefly examined the major techniques of forecasting, distinguishing between the two major categories of subjective or judgemental methods and the primarily mathe-matical objective techniques.

Chapter 14

Organisational Structures for Marketing

INTRODUCTION

Marketing within the organisation is accomplished by forming structural arrangements which direct marketing functions. These arrangements, for example, outline authority, responsibility and tasks which need to be performed; they also assign and co-ordinate tasks within the organisation. Such an organisation may be, for example:

❑ Functional, whereby responsibility is assigned on the basis of activities which need to be carried out, such as buying, selling, promotion, distribution, and so on.

❑ Product oriented, whereby managers are assigned to each product category, while individual brands are also given specific managers.

❑ Marketing-oriented, whereby managers are allocated different geographical areas or assigned particular types of customers.

Companies may be oriented in one or several of the above ways. The latest development, however, is towards marketing-oriented companies, whereby the over-arching concern for the organisation as a whole is the identification and satisfaction of customer needs.

In this chapter we shall look at how this marketing orientation can be achieved through the design of the organisational structure and systems for marketing, and the development of an appropriate culture in the marketing organisation. Without an appropriate organisational structure and culture, it is unlikely that even the best marketing plans can be implemented effectively.

THE DEVELOPMENT OF THE MARKETING-ORIENTED ORGANISATION

It used to be said that becoming 'marketing oriented' for many companies simply involved changing the sign on the sales manager's door to read 'Director of Marketing' and perhaps spending more on advertising. It is now generally agreed, however, that the benefits of subscribing to a 'complete marketing planning process' result in companies acquiring a significant competitive advantage. The marketing planning process is not just a series of procedural steps, but implies a whole value system, such as can only be sustained, it is claimed, by the culture of a 'mature organisation' composed of individuals who have experience and expertise which the organisation empowers them to employ. Clearly, if the requirements of the marketing-oriented organisation are to be fully carried through, great organisational changes will be needed for the majority of enterprises, including a far more dominant role for the marketing department.

There is, however, no simple formula which can be applied in all cases; the unique characteristics and circumstances confronting an enterprise, coupled with the dynamic nature of the change process itself, may require a number of different decisions for the firm, and result in an organisation which represents compromises and accommodation to these factors.

All firms that become marketing oriented, however, are subject to a number of broad changes. The time perspective of the firm moves towards a longer term; there is also a preoccupation with planning, since the firm must focus on the needs of consumers in order to produce the products which satisfy them, with the correct marketing mix to meet their needs over the long term, and the service to back this up.

Advocates of the marketing approach argue that the pursuit of these objectives involves every member of the company concerned, such is the depth of commitment required. Inevitably, the organisational structure of the company concerned will be transmuted.

Companies which concentrate on sales are much more likely to be divided into specialist departments, determined by the functions which this kind of organisation needs to carry out. Each department is likely to act in isolation to a certain extent, interacting with customers, for example, merely in terms of the priorities set by the nature of the specialist function with which it is concerned.

Marketing orientation demands, as a minima, that these priorities should be co-ordinated carefully around a central objective of achieving customer satisfaction. The basis of this approach, then, must be the predominance of the marketing department.

Conflicts are bound to occur in this situation – it is one thing to propose the idea of marketing 'obsession', but quite another to see the practical consequences for sections and individuals within an enterprise who suddenly find themselves subordinate to the activities and policies of the marketing department.

In practice, marketing departments work within very different kinds of practical constraints, according to the nature of the industry in which they operate, or to the history and circumstances of a particular firm. For each area of activity, changing to a marketing orientation will tend to move the firm towards a particular type of approach. The sales department will move away from a very inwardly focused 'live and die by short-term results' approach, towards a longer time focus, considering the needs and responsibilities of the organisation as a whole and concentrating on meeting customer needs. Purchasing looks towards an expanded horizon of activity, against the 'hermetic' tendency of specialists, while finance typically moves away from rigid cost accounting towards more creative and flexible arrangements. The name of the marketing game here is flexibility and responsiveness. The company which moves towards the marketing orientation commits itself to working in a particular way, focusing ever more precisely on well-targeted groups, and bending over backwards to satisfy the precise needs of the customer.

We are moving away from mass production, since we are also moving away from the pursuit of mass markets. Long production runs of restricted product ranges are being replaced by short production runs of a wider range of goods, which offer a range of options to the target groups. The dynamic nature of this system cannot be overemphasised, however, and, as we shall see, organisations are constantly struggling to reconcile the demands of this fragmented and diverse marketplace with the organisational problems posed by the

> In the marketing-oriented organisation, customer satisfaction is at the heart of its business philosophy: everything must be done to produce the products and services which satisfy the customer.

pursuit of excellence, while using human resources in the most effective manner possible.

ORGANISATIONAL STRUCTURES

What are organisations seeking to achieve? First, they serve to link individuals together in terms of specified roles and formally to fix the nature of authority (who has power, how much and so on), responsibility (who is required to 'get things done') and communications (who talks to whom and who knows what). Organisations usually specify the tasks that need to be carried out and group people together to get them done. They allocate rewards and sanctions, and the power to use them, so that these tasks and the overall objectives of the organisation can be achieved. Organisations also seek to accomplish these ends in the most efficient, effective and parsimonious manner by developing systems which establish a stable and successful set of processes and procedures which control and expedite the work which members have to carry out.

Organisations offer a way of getting complex things done, harmonising the activities of large and sometimes diverse groups and individuals. The organisation sets the terms under which people relate to each other by providing a structure which is composed of formally defined roles which tell members who they are within the set-up, who are their subordinates, and from whom they should take their orders. The establishment of norms, recurrent procedures, precedents and rules allows the ability to 'programme' decision-taking – individual variability is thus minimised. This offers stability and predictability so that decisions can be more confidently taken and plans formulated. The needs of the organisation – for example, for information or material resources – can be better planned, and individuals within the organisation, hopefully, will find it more satisfying and fulfilling.

The actual design of the organisation is likely to be influenced by a number of key dimensions: *Size* is one of the most important. An increasing scale means greater complexity and, consequently, necessary subdivision and specialisation. Control and co-ordination also become more difficult as communication channels get longer and more complex.

The form of the organisation is also influenced by the *nature of the tasks* which are involved in its work; related work may well be grouped together to make use of material resources or special skills, for example. Human Resource Management, in fact, also influence the way the organisation develops; skills levels, for example, will be related to the level of direction and supervision required.

Environmental factors will also influence the way in which the organisation is set up. Laws can be a problem or a boon for an organisation, while the commercial environment (the availability of investment capital, for example) will also affect issues such as the rate of growth. Clearly, too, technology will affect staffing levels, specialist skills needed, and the kinds of media which can be employed in the promotional aspects of the marketing plan.

Historical factors will often create a legacy around which the organisation will have to work. This can affect any aspect of the organisation's work – for example, firms now working in Eastern Europe find many aspects of the former Communist regimes still heavily influenced by the commercial, cultural, economic and political activities of the societies in which they exist.

Organisations themselves have a history, of course. Often, this can be positive (for example, a proud role in the pioneering of an industry), but it an also be negative (outdated working practices enshrined as 'traditions').

The organisation's *culture and style of management* adopted within the workplace may also be important factors in the development of the organisation. Often, traditions act as an important basis for loyalty and commitment within an organisation, and should be considered carefully when changes are contemplated. Likewise, styles of management can have an important impact on the way in which employees relate to the organisation – 'leadership' qualities are rare and valuable, and can be an important organisational resource.

When structures are being set up, they can be organised on the following bases:

Functions

In a manufacturing organisation, these might include marketing (in the marketing-oriented company), finance or general administration. The main virtue of this approach is its common-sense, logical appeal, and the fact that it is long established and familiar. Specialists fit easily into this framework, but the main problems arise in conflicts between those who may be concerned with overlapping roles when they address the same area – conflicts that arise between so-called 'line' and 'staff' functions. Specialisation into functions also creates communication difficulties and tends to encourage a defensive, parochial attitude which can inhibit the achievement of the overall aims of the firm.

Territory

If operations are widely dispersed but involve similar sorts of activities, there may well be a case for setting up an organisation which is organised around territories. Sales functions have traditionally run along these lines. This results in excellent feedback and the effective use of personal knowledge, but again communications and conflicts between personnel involved in overlapping areas of activity are the main drawback.

Products

Grouping around products is very common since the value of 'ownership' of a particular brand or product area by one or a team of managers enables the most effective monitoring and response to the particular problems and opportunities presented by the individual strategic business unit (SBU), the importance of which was discussed in Chapter 2. The owner can develop powerful expertise, pursue the most effective policy for the profitability of the individual brand, and bring together otherwise disparate activities for the good of marketing the product. It is, however, a costly system and the potentialities for conflicts between managers attempting to call on the resources of the firm all at the same time are obvious.

Customer/target market

This would seem to fit well with the emphasis on marketing effort and is regularly pursued in areas where high value purchases are involved (for instance, in industrial marketing). This also facilitates 'cross selling' by virtue of contact with, and knowledge about, customers and their needs, and promotes a 'customer care' ethos which is very important for a firm.

Technologies/processes

These often have a strong impact on organisational structure if a particular kind of resource is necessarily centralised or free-standing because of the cost or practical impossibility of duplication or access problems.

More recently, attention has turned to the 'matrix structure' as a form of organisation which can possibly resolve many of these problems. This involves setting up managers who are concerned with bringing together resources from different parts of an organisation in order to expedite and respond to customer needs in specific projects.

Functional departments remain, with heads responsible for their operation, but for each specific project, team co-ordinators take overall responsibility for those aspects of the functional departments' work which affect the project. Teams appear and disappear according to the needs of the organisation. This is a highly flexible and responsive system, gearing the capacities of specialists to the needs of customers much more effectively than functional teams. Because each project is 'owned', it also generates energy and commitment from managers, and fosters both co-operation and the 'empowerment' of individual team members who are drawn from what are often more traditional, hierarchical, department settings. It is a complex system, however; the possible conflicts between managers are built into the overlapping responsibilities which it cannot resolve effectively because of its fluidity, and there are clear risks for participants who must withdraw from the established systems, by means of which status and career prospects are built into the mainstream of the system. The culture of the organisation is a powerful mechanism and cannot be treated lightly. The matrix system disrupts the normal processes, to some degree, but the culture remains.

CULTURE IN THE MARKETING ORGANISATION

Every organisation almost inevitably develops a culture, or a standard way of running its affairs. Understanding what is going on and interpreting it, is possible only to insiders who have learned about the 'way of life' which each organisation distinctively promotes. Organisational cultures are not simply random, but are the product of interaction between a whole range of factors, such as economic conditions, the nature of the organisation and what its 'core business' involves, the personality and style of the top personnel, the policies and philosophies they pursue, the nature of the employees, and how the work they do is organised. Managers, including marketers, create their own 'sub-culture' within the organisation, too, according to the philosophy which animates their own work, their expressed belief about the way in which the organisation is or should be run, and, of course, the 'relics' of the managerial role – the cars they drive, how they dress, the perquisites of office, and so on.

Culture may inhibit the pursuit of the marketing organisation's objectives or it may be harnessed in their service. Getting the various groups within an organisation to agree what the cultural values of the organisation should be is an essential prerequisite to working effectively together.

Unless culture is positively nurtured, it is likely to have deleterious effects in the organisation. A sense of goal or direction is needed to motivate and give purpose to the work that people do; members also need to feel that they are 'pulling in the same direction'. Shared norms and familiar rules encourage a feeling of security and stability, too, and when these values are missing, the work of the organisation suffers. Conflicts occur as rivalries are unable to find an acceptable means of expression; groups and individuals become insecure, inward-looking and focused on the immediate consequences of their own activities rather than seeing what they do as part of a larger whole. Morale suffers, managers begin to abdicate responsibility and all change comes to be seen as threatening, so staff become obstructive and unwilling. The inevitable consequence is recourse to draconian and rigid discipline to enforce employee compliance. Marketing inevitably flounders in the face of these problems since the positive virtues it wishes to promote are totally absent.

Positive cultures are an essential goal of marketing managers, therefore, since they serve to foster:

❑ Higher levels of motivation and satisfaction among organisational members.
❑ Greater degrees of flexibility and adaptability, as well as a more positive attitude to change.
❑ A more attractive and positive image which adds value to the products and services the company aims to market.

Policies which foster positive culture need to be organised carefully around managerial functions such as communication, leadership, effective rewards, recruitment and corporate image-making. The overall strategy must be formulated precisely and implemented in co-ordinated policies in these areas.

It is essential for marketing managers to create a positive organisation culture which benefits staff morale and motivation as well as creating an attractive product image.

EFFECTIVE ORGANISATION FOR MARKETING

Marketing in relation to the overall functioning of the organisation has assumed a more prominent role in a large number of organisations, as it is responsible for planning, resource allocation, monitoring and controlling the marketing plan. How is this role to be continued in the most effective way? As we have just seen, the development of a positive organisational culture is an essential prerequisite of successful marketing. One of the ways in which this has been systematically pursued is through the strategy of 'internal marketing' or the development of 'quality chains'. Quality and marketing orientation seem to be part of the same philosophy and are often discussed together.

Quality, it can be argued, is meeting the requirements of the consumer, and, whatever business we are in, there are the relations of 'supplier-customer' which can be seen as a series of quality chains. Customers are inside as well as outside organisations.

It is now argued that meeting customer requirements is the main focus in the search for quality, while these requirements would typically include aspects such as availability, delivery, reliability, maintainability and cost effectiveness. The first priority, in fact, is to establish what customer requirements actually are. If the customer is outside the organisation, then the supplier must seek to set up a marketing activity to gather this information, and to relate the output of their organisation to the needs of the customer. Customers inside the organisation who require services are equally important, but seldom are their requirements investigated. The quality implementation process requires that all the supplier customer relationships within the quality chain should be treated as marketing exercises, and that each customer should be carefully consulted as to their precise requirements from the product or service with which they are to be provided.

Market research must be set up to establish the exact requirement of the customer, so that only the highest standards of service and customer care are provided by the organisation.

This approach is only one in a burgeoning area of competing theories which share a common vocabulary of 'customer care', 'service' and 'quality'. Underlying them all, arguably, is the customer orientation which marketing planning seeks to apply. As we have seen, the development of these approaches is dynamic and will doubtless continue to change according to the interaction of environmental factors which has brought them into being in the first instance.

Summary

In this chapter we have examined the importance of designing an appropriate structure for the marketing organisation. This structure must not only enable the marketer to implement plans effectively but perhaps more importantly, it should help to develop a marketing/customer orientation in the company. Because of this it is not only structure and procedures which need to be marketing oriented, but also the organisational culture has to be one which is built around customers. There are a variety of ways of organising the marketing function, each of which has advantages and limitations. A number of factors affect the choice of organisational structure, but overall the structure must be such as to facilitate the implementation of plans based on putting customer needs at the centre of the organisation and all its activities.

Chapter 15

Organisational Development

INTRODUCTION

Clearly, strategic marketing plans cannot be implemented effectively unless the very concept of the need for a strategic approach to marketing has been accepted throughout the organisation. It has been shown that the necessity of adopting a strategic approach to marketing planning is now generally accepted by most pundits. As we saw earlier, the need for a strategic approach is due to a number of reasons, some of which are discussed below.

As the production of goods has proliferated during the age of mass production and mass markets, eventually many markets have become saturated. Consequently, competition in overcrowded marketplaces between larger numbers of products and services has become a desperate search for a product attribute which offers the key competitive advantage to attract the attention and purchase activity of the ever-more discerning and sophisticated consumer. In this situation, as discussed in Chapter 14, a marketing orientation and a carefully planned mode of operation becomes essential for survival. We also saw that achieving a marketing orientation necessitates not only an appropriate organisational structure, but also an appropriate organisational culture. In this chapter we will explore in more detail the issues in developing such a culture and look in particular at the ways in which the requirement for substantial cultural change in the organisation can be achieved. We will also look at the key management functions which will need to become established within the organisation if it is to develop successfully a strategic approach to marketing planning. Finally, we will return to the important area of the marketing environment, but this time we will look at the effect of the environment on some of the ways in which organisations are approaching their marketing planning activities.

PROBLEMS AND OPPORTUNITIES IN ORGANISATIONAL CULTURE

Inertia must give way to radical organisational change if a culture which supports strategic marketing planning is to be effected.

Previous research has determined that many corporate cultures create an inertia which often stands in the way of attempts to introduce radical change when this is needed. It is now generally accepted that if change is to take place within an organisation, existing cultural norms have first to be loosened and their 'cultural carriers' discredited.

Within the organisation, various roles have to be played, such as:

❏ *Change agent*: the person who stimulates change from within the organisation, or as an external consultant.
❏ *Catalyst*: one with sufficient power to make certain that change actually does take place.
❏ *Pacemaker*: one who provides the energy to keep the change process going.
❏ *Diffusion agent*: one who helps to transfer or communicate the change into the furthest recesses of the organisation.

Individuals who play these roles assume different degrees of importance or prominence according to the stage in the process of change. Thus, 'change agents' are likely to be pre-eminent at the beginning of the process, but to give way to the 'pacemaker' and the 'diffusion agent' in the later stages.

Experts in the area of organisational change suggest that there are a number of different ways of intervening in a company in order to effect change. The type of intervention used and the degree of coercion involved depends on the strength of the existing culture. Research into how change is introduced identified five main actions which leaders take to transmit and embed a culture. These 'primary mechanisms' are:

❏ How the leader reacts to crises or critical incidents.

❑ The criteria they establish for allocating rewards or status.
❑ The areas to which the leader pays attention, measures and controls.
❑ The criteria they establish for recruitment, selection, promotion, retirement and dismissing staff.
❑ The role model the leader promotes by either their own behaviour or by coaching and teaching others.

Organisational change is also transmitted at other levels, including organisational systems and procedures, organisational design and structure, the design of physical spaces and environments, formal statements about organisational philosophy and ideas, and the history and mythology of the company and its heroes.

The key elements affecting the change process, however, are the culture which the company has developed and the actions of key powerful individuals in promoting the change process.

READINESS TO CHANGE

The desire to develop a strategic marketing planning approach is in itself an inadequate basis for achieving that aim. If an organisation is to make that change successfully, a whole range of conditions need to be satisfied. For example, the organisation must exhibit the following characteristics:

❑ Precise identification of target consumers.
❑ Good knowledge of their behaviour, attitudes, needs, wants, lifestyles, and so on.
❑ Profit rather than volume drive underlying its strategy.
❑ A market-driven mission.
❑ Marketing enthusiasts among the top management.
❑ Responsiveness, openness to change and the capacity to change in response to threats or opportunities.
❑ The ability to use marketing information and research data effectively in decision-making.
❑ Effective control and use of financial data.
❑ Effective linkages between marketing activity and product development processes.

❏ Effective use of marketing professionals within the organisation, as opposed to a sales driven culture.

❏ Marketing central to all organisational activities.

Strategic marketing planning can only be successfully introduced with care, together with a recognition that such profound changes are likely to be possible only over a longer time period. A change in core values is required, and this can only be successful when it is truly established in the basic culture of the organisation and not through something tantamount to a religious conversion. Change can be instituted systematically, however, and programmes for strategic change, necessarily, must go through a number of stages.

A change in core values can only be implemented with the support of top management.

The support of top management is clearly essential. For a company to change its core values is a profound change and appropriate programmes cannot be introduced successfully in a piecemeal fashion. Organisational change also needs to be rigorously formulated into a statement of corporate philosophy, with specific time related objectives attached to it. To succeed, both material and human resources need to be devoted specifically to the programme. Typically, this involves the establishment of a team which is given the specific brief to analysing the current state of the company, identifying appropriate forms and methods of change in the culture of the company, and formulating an appropriate series of actions, along with costings and recommendations for the institution of structural changes, in order to achieve the development of a strategic marketing system.

To establish and maintain momentum in this process, systems of monitoring and evaluation must also be established. These would establish ways of measuring the indicators of progress and effectiveness, such as customer satisfaction surveys, and bench-marks of effectiveness in, for example, product quality or delivery times.

Many of these systems are very close to the programmes of Quality Improvement or Total Quality Management (TQM) which have become extremely popular. The common thread is a focus on customers and attention to the features of the environment which are likely to be important in the success or otherwise of the firm – for example, competitor activity, socio-economic changes, and corporate culture.

ESTABLISHING THE KEY STRATEGIC MARKETING PLANNING MANAGEMENT FUNCTIONS

Cultural change and new core values are central to the establishment of strategic marketing planning within the organisation. To change the organisation so that this becomes an established system, however, requires that certain key management functions should become established within the organisation of the company. These are:

❑ Analysis.
❑ Planning.
❑ Implementation.
❑ Control.

Analysis

As we have seen in earlier chapters, analysis in the modern sense involves the systematic means to use the burgeoning amount of research information which is available to the modern marketer in order to examine the markets with which the company is concerned: how large are they? how profitable? how are they changing? why?; the activities of competitors and how these affect our strategic plans; the characteristics of our customers; and, of course, the position which our company occupies; how big is our market share? how do our different product ranges and brands contribute to the performance of the company? what is our profitability? and so on. All these areas can be effectively analysed in the modern world only by using marketing research techniques correctly, by gathering all the relevant marketing intelligence data, by employing the best forms of analytical tools and techniques, (which are increasingly common in the age of the micro-computer and the information superhighway) and finally, by disseminating the results, in a form which personnel throughout the enterprise will find relevant and useful to their concerns by the use of a modern marketing information system (MkIS), as discussed in Chapter 11.

Planning

The purpose of analysis, as we have seen, is to provide a basis on which marketing plans can be produced; if management science in general has a theme, it is the attempt to develop the capacity to make better decisions, and good analysis provides the information which can help us to do this. We have explored, of course, the key decisions which must be taken in the formulation of marketing plans, which include those which relate to objectives, product range, target markets, strategies and mix decisions.

Implementation

The process of putting the plans into practice has the most obvious direct consequences for the organisation. Organising for change here means committing staff, financial resources and effort into plans which take place within clear constraints of time, and involve the careful development of organisational structures, as discussed in Chapter 14, allocating responsibility and power in order to accomplish these ends.

Control

This relates to the idea of 'getting the work done' – how do we know if we are winning or losing? The obvious answer is to establish tests or checks which monitor how the organisation is doing, and measure the effectiveness or otherwise of the plans and strategies which it has put into place. This information then enters the 'analysis' stage of the planning cycle and so forms a 'looped programme', feeding back on itself.

CLASSIFYING FIRMS IN TERMS OF THEIR RESPONSE TO CHANGE

Much of what was said at the beginning of the chapter regarding the importance of cultural change related to the internal environment of the firm. The external environment, the main components of which were discussed in Chapter 3 in the context of the marketing audit, is also very important, however, and change necessarily comes about in the course of interaction with the so-called 'macro environment' or the firm will find itself in trouble. The Darwinian model of biological evolution is often employed in the commercial world in talking of 'the survival of the fittest', although recent evidence suggests that Darwin developed the model as a result of the influence of Adam Smith's economic theories of competition within the marketplace!

As we saw in Chapter 3, the environment of the firm is probably more dynamic now than at any time in the past, as the economies of the world merge into a global marketplace. The issue for firms is how to respond appropriately to change not just to enable the firm to survive, but to attempt to anticipate and capitalise on the way in which change takes place – to be a market leader rather than follow in a direction which has been set by others or has emerged out of what some writers have referred to as the 'chaos' of the modern marketplace.

Three main types of organisation can be discerned in terms of their capacity to react to change factors within the macro environment.

1. Those which appreciate and understand the forces which produce change, and so are able to react correctly and even to influence change in some instances.
2. Those which fail to react promptly enough to the change process, and are forced to react constantly to change forces simply to survive.
3. Those which are oblivious, ignorant or unreactive to change, and constantly suffer the consequences of, at best, poor profits, and, at worst, extinction.

MARKETING VARIABLES AND THE MACRO ENVIRONMENT

Capitalist economies, particularly those which operate under 'free market' conditions and are subject only to very limited areas of state direction and control, are free to design and implement plans which cover very large amounts of manufacturing and marketing activity. Products and services are subject to constraints in some areas (for instance, there are laws commonly governing the safety of many items, and the use of processes and ingredients which are judged to involve unacceptable risks for customers or workers in the manufacturing process and are banned or closely regulated), but there are, nevertheless, high degrees of freedom concerning what may be produced or offered for sale. Likewise, the process of marketing enables the firm itself to decide the price of its products, and to formulate policies about promotion, packaging and distribution, which are a mixture of commercial objectives and responsiveness to the laws and social norms of the society in which the products are to be offered for sale.

Of course, these decisions are not plucked from the air, but are strongly affected by the circumstances within which the firm offers its products to the marketplace. Again, as we discussed in Chapter 3, the wider environment which influences the firm is commonly described in terms of four types of factors, the so-called PEST or STEP variables:

❑ Political.
❑ Economic.
❑ Socio-cultural.
❑ Technological.

Closer to home, the firm is strongly influenced by the factors which dominate its conditions of operation – more precisely, by the element discussed in Chapter 4, namely, its competitive environment. Remember, the competitive environment includes firms which offer direct competition in the form of alternative or substitute products, and those which offer products which may not be direct substitutes in the sense of providing the same satisfactions or possessing comparable characteristics, but which may compete for the same disposable income or time commitment. Suppliers may also be said to constitute an environmental factor, and this poses severe organisational problems in some industries. It is crucial to ensure a supply of raw materials at a price which affords the possibility of profitable margins for the final product, but there are also issues about the costs involved in, for instance, stockholding. The Japanese have pioneered a new way of operating between the firm and its suppliers, drawing suppliers into contracts which require them to meet very high standards of quality and reliability in delivery. This permits the manufacturer to operate a 'just-in-time' (JIT) system of stockholding (referred to on page 122), in which stockholding is kept to an absolute minimum,

High standards of customer service can be achieved through the 'just-in-time' system of stockholding.

avoiding the costs involved. Some car manufacturers now hold no stock whatsoever, yet still offer better delivery times for vehicles which are manufactured precisely to meet the requirements of the individual customer than firms which operate traditional systems within the same industry. This system of manufacturing is now termed 'lean manufacturing'. Finally, the operating conditions include the environment within which the firm itself makes its product available, the distributive environment. This includes middlemen, such as agents, distributors, factors, wholesalers, and so on. There are big changes afoot in this area too, as more and more firms are following the example set by industrial marketers and selling direct to their customers, using the possibilities afforded by new electronic media for communicating with, and keeping detailed records for, widely dispersed individuals.

This new approach to selling is sometimes called 'database marketing', and it is revolutionising many areas of marketing. There is no doubt that database marketing is having profound consequences on both the way that marketers approach their task (increasingly using market research data to identify precise target markets and database information to keep track of purchases so that 'cross selling' can take place), and on the ability of small enterprises to compete globally with much larger competitors (since it affords them the possibility of identifying and meeting needs, and also of changing products to meet fluctuating tastes). The key point here, however, is that some theorists have argued that the whole shape of organisations is being transformed by these factors. For example, 'delayering' is taking place, in which entire sections of middle management are simply removed. This is possible because the primary function of the individuals in these layers was to gather, record, store and transmit information to those above and below them. In the modern firm, these tasks are accomplished, to a large extent, by management information systems.

Database marketing is having a revolutionary effect, enabling precise target marketing to take place, improving sales methods and achieving global competition.

Summary

In this chapter we have looked at the importance and the issues in managing organisational change in order to bring about a culture which supports a strategic approach to marketing planning. We have also looked at the key management functions which need to be established for a strategic approach. Finally, we have once again looked at the marketing environment and the impact which this has on how a company approaches its marketing planning and activities.

Chapter 16
Contingency Planning

INTRODUCTION

In this chapter we will look again at the complexity and instability of the environment, and the degree to which this can be accommodated and counteracted by strategic marketing planning. As we saw in Chapter 12, marketing mix factors are largely controllable by the marketer, but marketing takes place within a setting filled with contingent factors. These are vitally important since any marketing plan is likely to fail if it is adversely affected by such factors. In order to minimise the impact which these are likely to have, it is important that we develop appropriate contingency plans which relate to these uncontrollable variables that enter the planning process, and that these contingency plans are incorporated into the overall marketing plan.

Contingency planning aims to force managers to think ahead and to consider the possibility that things may go wrong, and in that eventuality, to question what they will do.

HOW FLEXIBLE IS THE STRATEGY WHICH IS BEING PURSUED?

Strategies which make risky assumptions about how things are likely to turn out in the real world are a bad idea, unless they also include plans about what to do if something happens to affect the success of the main strategy. Any marketing plan, and the organisation for which it is intended, therefore, needs to be looked at in terms of the following:

❏ The capacity to respond to changes in the operating environment. This relates not just to the overall capacity of the organisation to react, but also to specific features, such as the speed of reaction, and the effects of this response upon the resources and personnel of the organisation.

❏ The changes which would be needed for the organisation to avert crisis or to offset the partial failure to meet objectives. In other words, what effect would partial or complete failure in this strategy have upon the overall operational effectiveness of the organisation? Can any safeguards or 'fail-safe' mechanisms be built into the strategic marketing planning process?

❏ Those options or alternatives which are available to the organisation, given assumptions about particular changes. All options need to be fully analysed and evaluated so that they can be integrated, if feasible, into the final strategic marketing plan.

VARIABLES WHICH GIVE RISE TO THE NEED FOR CONTINGENCY PLANS

Given that contingency plans are about planning for changes in the environment which may affect marketing plans and the assumptions on which they are based, not surprisingly the main variables which give rise to the need for contingency plans are broadly the same environment variables which we discussed under the marketing audit stage of developing the marketing plan in Chapters 3 and 4. However, rather than look at these variables from the point of view of assessing opportunities and threats, in this chapter we shall consider how these variables affect contingency planning. In addition to some of the environmental variables that were outlined in these earlier chapters, we have also added another key variable which affects contingency plans – namely, mass communications media:

❏ Customers.
❏ Competition.
❏ The political environment.
❏ The legal environment.
❏ The economic environment.

❏ Technological change.
❏ Mass communications media.

Customers

As discussed in Chapter 7, marketing plans identify and target a particular group of consumers, but marketers cannot control the characteristics of those consumers, of course. The age group, income group, occupation, ethnicity, and so on, of the consumers cannot be controlled by the marketer who must accept customers' characteristics and constantly aim to identify and respond to the ways in which these characteristics change. Thus, for instance, the ways in which customers choose products or the criteria which they apply in evaluating them, may appear irrational, but it is dangerous and inappropriate to try to 'educate' consumers about what they should do. 'The customer', the marketer must remember, 'is always right.' Thus, for instance, customers may believe that weight or colour, for example, are signs of quality or value – for instance, in the case of food products or textiles – while specialists know better because of their technical expertise or scientific training. Plans must be based on what customers believe, however, otherwise they will fail.

In addition, of course, consumers are subject to influence. Any changes in these influencing factors can have a major effect on customers' choice and their specific needs and wants. Thus it is important to prepare contingency plans in the event that any major influencing factors may change. For example, a key influencing factor on customer choice may be reference groups, such as family, opinion leaders, influencers, and so. A change in reference group influence may give rise to the need for changes in marketing plans. For example, if a famous footballer changes to another brand of football boot, this may in turn be reflected in the purchase choice of customers who are influenced by the particular sporting personality.

Be prepared to change marketing plans when customers decide to change their choice of product.

Competition

The importance of competitor analysis was outlined in Chapter 4 where it was shown that competitors have a strong influence on the marketing strategy pursued by a firm. We examined some of the key areas of competitor analysis, including, for example, the importance of assessing the strengths and weaknesses of competitors, their likely strategies and responses, and so on. In addition to the elements of competitor analysis, when developing contingency plans it can also be useful to analyse the competitive structure which the firm is facing. Here the more conventional notions of competitive market structure developed by economists can be used. The four main structures identified by the economists are:

❏ Monopoly (one firm selling a particular good or service).
❏ Oligopoly (few firms, generally large, comprising most of an industry's sales).
❏ Monopolistic competition (several large firms, each offering a unique marketing mix).
❏ Pure competition (many firms selling identical products or services).

Once the nature of the market has been determined, the marketing structures of competitors need to be worked out in order to identify opportunities in the form of 'gaps', but also to spot cases where markets are overpopulated and, consequently, saturated. The marketing plans of competitors, including the target markets which they aim to reach, how they intend to 'position' their products, what brand personalities are being created and the other sorts of 'competitive advantage' enjoyed, along with customer reactions to and perceptions of competitors – all these aspects of competitor activity need to be taken into account in the development of contingency planning. Since the relationship with competitors is dynamic, then our policies will produce a response in competitors, of course, so that contingency planning assumes a 'game' quality – 'If I do this, what will my competitors do?'

In the context of developing contingency plans, channel relationships are also an important part of the competitive environment. Good relations with retailers and the guarantee of advantageous shelf space and in store positioning are obviously vitally important for successful marketing plans. Maintaining good relations or obtaining good channel relations upon market entry are key factors for the marketing manager, and must be a high priority in any contingency plan.

Maintaining good relations with retailers is of vital importance in the development of contingency plans.

Contingency planning also needs to take into account the ways in which relations with competitors change as a consequence of new tastes or changes in behaviour. Thus, for example, what count as competitive products may well change over time – in the world of fashion, for example, 'specialist' markets (for outdoor clothing, or products associated with just one sex group) may suddenly become competitive with general or mass-market products as a result of fashion changes.

The political environment

The operating conditions which face a firm, affecting every aspect of its operation, from the conditions of workers to the disposal of waste after it has been consumed, are such an obvious and vital feature of the conditions of operation that any firm must try to accommodate them within its contingency planning.

Often, government institutions provide grants and other sorts of incentives – for example, preferential interest rates or free loans which enable the firm to operate – and strongly influence the kinds of marketing plans which are used.

The laws and general conditions under which the firm may operate will be affected by the political environment. Recent examples would include the increased power of consumer organisations and political views on the private ownership of the utilities, such as water and electricity. Mobilisation of public opinion in one direction or another will produce tangible changes in the environment and have a strong impact on the marketing plan. Contingency planning must monitor and, as far as possible, try to anticipate changes in this environment.

The economic environment

Plans to market products in any part of the world must take account of the economic situation which prevails. Growth in the economy, based on measures such as the gross national product (GNP) which indicates the annual volume of goods and services produced, will provide indications for the likely consequences in different sectors of the economy. A slowdown in, for example, manufacturing goods or housebuilding will have a knock-on effect on the disposable income available to purchase consumer goods and services. Strong growth is usually a reliable indicator of a healthy demand for consumer goods and services.

Consumer confidence is another key area. Perceiving the economy as strong, stable and settled will increase the propensity of consumers to spend the money they have rather than to save it in case times become harder or they lose their job.

The costs of doing business, such as the price of raw materials, wage rates, interest rates, property charges, and so on, which are beyond the control of planners within an organisation, are all dimensions which need to be incorporated into the contingency planning process. These are the typical areas which concern the marketing planner, since high inflation or unemployment will almost certainly produce a cut-back on certain types of consumption. A key measure in this regard is the fate of 'real income', that is to say, an indexed measure of what people are earning, adjusted according to some 'base' figure so that inflationary effects are taken into account. This is the true measure of what people are likely to have to spend on particular products, since the 'cash' figure for earnings takes no account of the way in which other prices have risen. Likewise, unemployed people as consumers tend to reduce drastically their spending on luxuries, although, of course, what counts as a luxury and what are necessities certainly changes from place to place and from time to time. In certain areas, cars are likely to be counted as a necessity because of the difficulty of reaching certain key resources, such as shopping centres, hospitals or schools.

TECHNOLOGICAL CHANGE

The machines, products and processes involved in the process of marketing certainly change dramatically from time to time, and many of these are far beyond the control of the individual or the firm. For instance, the development of small, cheap personal computers has had a dramatic effect on the way in which we work, shop, entertain ourselves, carry out different sorts of tasks, and also, of course, the way we play. New products with a huge competitive advantage may suddenly transform even the most long-established and stable markets and their planners – for example, the digital watch, colour television and the compact disk.

Contingency planning may address these sorts of issues in a number of different ways – for instance, firms which develop such products will seek to protect their competitive advantage by using patents, where applicable, although these have a limited time-span. Nevertheless, the protection they provide enables planning to assume limits on the range of competition which is likely.

Where copycat products come on to the market, contingency planning needs to be aware of the dangers which are involved and incorporate the appropriate monitoring procedures so that the necessary responses to this strategy can be produced: For example, legal action may be taken to protect 'intellectual copyright' – for instance, where 'copy' products use logos, brand names, packaging design or product formats which capitalise on the brand leader's popularity – or marketing strategic action may be applied to reposition the product to establish its distinctiveness in the face of its competitors.

Mass communications media (non-promotional)

The mass media play a vital part in many aspects of marketing planning programmes, and here the effect which they have is under the control of the marketer. But large parts of the media may influence the success or failure of marketing strategies which are not controlled by the company, and they may well influence the ways in which the government, consumers and a whole range of different publics view the company, its operations, the products or services it offers and even its personnel. Negative publicity in any of these areas or related to any of these publics can have potentially devastating consequences for the company or its products. Recent examples are food scares that involve various products which have been severely affected by media coverage of the health risks associated with consuming these products; similarly, negative stories about the conditions in which animals are reared as part of modern food production have had a significant impact on sales and also produced hostile political reactions which have made it difficult to obtain support for particular sorts of legislation which affects the way in which animals are transported, for example. Other negative stories in the uncontrolled media have highlighted high levels of pay in some boardrooms, in companies which have imposed severe pay restraints on low-level staff and made significant reductions within the workforce. This can form the basis for hostile political reactions and has led, in some cases, to customer boycott and a bad corporate image which competitors may seek to exploit.

In some cases, a flamboyant or a high-profile CEO can have a very positive impact, contributing to the personality of the brand and giving consumers extra confidence or reassurance about the quality of the company's products. A CEO overreaching him or herself can have a cataclysmic impact, however, as in the famous case of an injudicious joke made at an after-dinner speech by the managing director of a hugely successful jewellery chain who compared the durability of his products to the prawn sandwiches being served.

Effective contingency planning can turn a possible disaster into a positive advantage and produce a long-term success.

Although the uncontrolled media are not a source of advertising, contingency planning will make sure that there are channels which can be used and strategies which can be employed through public relations activities to sustain a favourable image of the company, or to repair damage which may occur as a result of publicity being given to negative stories. Effective contingency planning in this instance can sometimes turn a problem into an opportunity – in the case of the Perrier company, for example, negative coverage over unfavourable ingredients in its product was turned into long-term success because the company accepted the problem ('owned' it), took extensive, expensive and very high-profile remedial action, including massive withdrawal of the product, and gave great publicity to what it was doing to take care of customers' safety and to assure product quality.

Summary

Contingency planning, then, covers a large number of issues within the marketing environment and may require many different kinds of actions. It is undoubtedly true, however, that such planning is becoming more important in the developing global economy, but also that it is becoming more and more difficult to identify areas in which contingencies are likely to arise.

Chapter 17

Plan Reviews: Strategic Controls and The Evaluation Process

INTRODUCTION

As essential part of effective strategic marketing planning is the assessment of how well or how badly, our plans are working. This chapter looks at the control and evaluation of marketing plans. We shall discuss how the strategic marketing planning process itself acts as a form of control mechanism, but then we shall move on to the control process and the various forms which that control may take. How to develop progress reviews for the marketing plan and some of the major tools of control, such as customer tracking, and the marketing audit, will also be discussed.

THE FUNCTIONS OF THE MARKETING PLAN

The planning process, as we have seen, is framed in different forms, with differential degrees of detail, according to the scope of the plan, and according to the concerns and responsibilities of the managers involved. Corporate strategic planning, then, tends to have a very broad focus, encompassing many different areas on a longer time-scale, and, as a consequence, cannot operate to control and monitor all the detailed and short-term 'micro' events and processes which make up the operational reality of a commercial enterprise.

Short-term marketing planning (and the significance of 'short term' may be quite different in disparate markets), in so far as it is possible to generalise, refers to between 3 and 12 months ahead. How far short-term marketing plans are possible depends on the capacity to identify separate markets and to differentiate separate products. It also depends on the knowledge which we can use to make good decisions and how easy or difficult this is to obtain, along with the personnel that we can devote to this planning process.

Short-term marketing planning is usually done under the brand management system which is commonly used by companies selling, for example, fast-moving consumer goods (FMCG). As competition has increased in modern markets and the penalties for failure have grown, the need for detailed planning and the employment of sophisticated and careful approaches to marketing has become much more widely accepted. Top management within an organisation now expects detailed plans for the activities related to the marketing plan, and, providing a plan such as this functions as a major control mechanism. It serves principally:

❑ To synchronise corporate activity.
❑ To justify expenditure on marketing activities.
❑ To provide a résumé of marketing assumptions and of the state of the market.
❑ To present a review of the actual levels of marketing competence within the organisation.

Presenting the annual marketing plan, then, provides a thorough review of the company's products and details the way in which the marketing planning function is intended to operate. It functions as a control, by providing a point of reference or a bench-mark. ✘

More detailed controls are extremely important, however, and a review of the marketing plan must also incorporate various 'control dynamics'. In general, control processes function to make sure that management achieves its goals in terms of the actions or stages which have been formulated as the marketing strategy, taking into account the contingencies and known constraints affecting the capacity of the organisation to carry out its plans. As the above characterisation of the control function of the marketing plan indicates, however, the

Presentation of the annual marketing plan is an important point of reference to review the company's products and marketing strategy.

processes of planning and control are intimately interconnected and are complementary to each other.

Control may take two basic forms:

❑ *Open loop*, in which errors are neither monitored nor corrected.
❑ *Closed loop*, in which feedback derived from checks, tests and observations are related to the objectives of the organisation.

The latter is also referred to as a 'marketing planning control system' (MPCS).

Control dynamics in the MPCS rest on the establishment of certain procedures within the organisation. These involve:

❑ The development of performance criteria and standards.
❑ The development of acceptable ranges within which these criteria and standards will be deemed to have been satisfied.
❑ Developing procedures which will provide suitable and reliable measures of results.
❑ Developing the means actually to compare results achieved with standards set.
❑ Developing systems which enable effective corrective measures to be taken.
❑ Developing a trustworthy means of forecasting outcomes.

An overview of the nature of the control process is shown in Figure 17.1.

Marketing planning controls fall into three broad types: system controls, procedural controls and performance standards.

System controls include a number of explicitly established control elements and also some related procedures which contribute towards this function – for example, the cycle of control which is part of the planning process operates in this way. System controls in themselves include:

❑ The marketing information system.
❑ The budgetary control system.
❑ Periodic plan reviews, within fixed planning horizons.
❑ The human activity system of management control which designs, implements and operates the system.

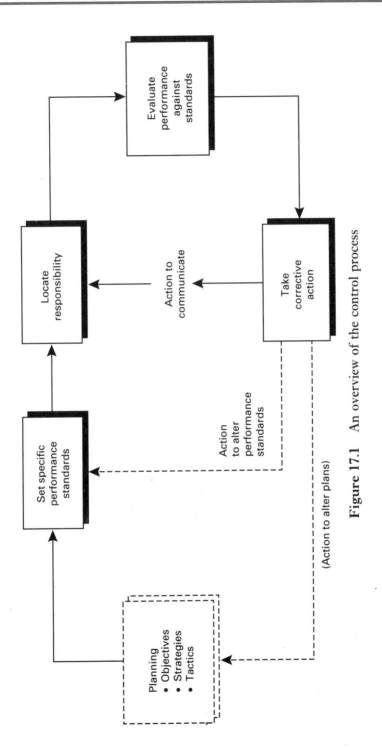

Figure 17.1   An overview of the control process

The latter also, of course, includes the functions of top management who are involved in regulating and operating the control system itself.

Procedural controls comprise three main types. Those which are concerned with the planning sequence over time – that is, those relating to annual and rolling plans; those which take place at a fixed interval and may involve revising objectives in the light of contingencies which typically take place at monthly or quarterly intervals; and the more general system of monitoring itself, which will include the means by which measures and tests can be applied to check on how well the marketing plan is proceeding.

Performance standards of the kind which are so important to quality system maintenance, are an essential part of the control system. In the case of both goods and services, these comprise 'bench-marks' whereby how the organisation is actually performing in relation to the objectives of the marketing plan is set against projected measures of performance – for example, production figures – or the costs and profits which were estimated (a budgetary measure). It is highly desirable that, wherever possible, such measures should be quantified and robust so that they give a true and, if possible, objective measure of performance. Inevitably, however, there are some measures of performance which must be qualitative since they depend on impressions and feelings – for instance, customer reactions to certain aspects of sales techniques or advertising.

CONTROL PROCEDURES

Control procedures are essential to evaluate performance in terms of the objectives of the strategic marketing plan.

The central notion involved in the control sequence, then, is that some measures, whether quantitative or qualitative, can be taken which will serve to evaluate performance at various levels. More specifically, this evaluation will be in terms of the objectives of the strategic marketing plan and the effectiveness of the tactics employed in pursuit of strategic marketing plan objectives. The control sequence asks questions such as:

❏ What has happened with regard to the marketing plan?
❏ How does this accord with the time-scale or programme indicated by the marketing plan?

❑ How does this measure up to our intended progress?
❑ Why has this happened?
❑ What costs have been incurred?
❑ How does this fit into our budgeted figures?
❑ What actions are required as a result of this?

It is essential that these questions should relate to clearly delineated responsibility centres – that is, a part of the organisation, such as a cost centre, a profit centre or an investment centre, which recognises itself as a distinct operational unit, with clear responsibilities and delimited spheres of activity, including personnel who can be delegated 'to make things happen'; in other words, a part of the company with considerable autonomy in important areas.

MARKETING PLAN PROGRESS REVIEWS

Keeping tabs on the degree to which budgeted targets for each product within the corporate portfolio have been realised – measured by value and volume – usually takes place month by month. The progress towards the achievement of the 'bottom line' – the projected corporate revenue, expenditure and profits – is obviously a central concern of the most senior personnel within an organisation, and a system must be established which enables them to do this as a matter of routine, producing reliable and useful data as and when it is needed. This comes primarily from the accounting system, but in order to monitor the progress of the marketing plan effectively, other sorts of criteria must be met:

❑ Data must be available at the appropriate level – aggregated performance figures for product types will give little or no reliable indication about the performance of individual brands within the portfolio.
❑ Profit responsibilities need to be clearly delineated – for instance, a clearly specified profit responsibility for the marketing function will encourage accountability in the performance of individual brands, product types, and so on.
❑ Continued shortfalls against projected performance should trigger revision or remedial activity.

❏ Plan review meetings can also function as occasions on which certain kinds of information can be disseminated, particularly marketing research data which may well have been commissioned on behalf of one section and may not easily 'trickle across' to others.

At the corporate level, a whole range of related functions may be served by the review of the marketing plan and its effectiveness. The strong focus in reviews at this level is on volume and price so that targeted sales volume can be achieved with a given price level. This reflects the concern of corporate officers whose primary concern is with return to shareholders. It is the key function of marketing, as many corporate officers see it, to control the price and the sales volume level in such a way that profit objectives can be realised. Certainly, variable costs, such as raw materials, labour or promotional media, are not controllable, so that constant monitoring is necessary in order to make the fine adjustments which are necessary to remain on target. This requires a constant flow of accurate and reliable information from the marketing information system (MkIS). If this is available, the monitoring process can be routinised.

Corporate controls will also operate over new product development, with specific reviews of the development of such products or services. These controls serve as a stimulus to the development of new products. In particular, the responsibility of the marketing function within an organisation is its contribution to this process. Since the marketing function has as its primary focus the needs of identified target consumers, clearly it must be central to the development of new product lines.

STRATEGIC CONTROLS AND MARKETING CONTROLS

While many of the evaluation and review procedures which relate to the marketing plan operate at the corporate level, it is also the case that strategic controls operate within marketing planning departments. The systems instituted by the marketing function typically relate to the way in which the objectives and responsibilities of the department are handled, to ensure that administrative responsibilities are dealt with properly, and that those whose aim is to ensure that the activities with which the department is concerned in the marketplace itself, achieve all that they possibly can – in other words, making sure that the department performs its optimum role within the corporate structure.

The control process overall can be said to have four main aims:

1. To permit problems – that is, developments which do not match planned or budgeted schedules – to be identified early and regularly.
2. To identify their causes and act to nullify their effects.
3. To provide input into the ongoing marketing function of identifying marketing opportunities and threats.
4. To act as a performance indicator and stimulus for marketing personnel.

The process involves a logical continuum, starting with the determination of what needs to be controlled – for example, sales, costs, and profits, but also the marketing objectives and strategies set – then establishing control objectives – financial or relative to volume, as stated earlier. The sequence then moves through the setting of performance standards, specifying the measures to be applied, and culminating in the analysis of results and the establishment of feedback routines which enable remedial action to be instituted in accordance with the results obtained.

The key areas for control in marketing are quite distinct from each other. Different approaches are used, different purposes and different areas of responsibility are entailed in each of the areas listed below:

❏ *Annual plan control*, as we have seen, is the remit of top management and examines performance in relation to planned results.
❏ *Profit control* is the specific responsibility of the marketing controller and aims to see how each product fits into the overall performance of the corporate portfolio – in other words, what is making money and what is not.
❏ *Efficiency control* is managed by line and staff management, and examines ways of improving marketing efficiency. How can the

salesforce work more effectively? How good is our advertising? Does it do what we intend it to do?

❑ *Strategic control* which aims to evaluate overall marketing planning and implementation systems, is the concern of top management. It seeks to examine the effectiveness of marketing and to carry out marketing audits.

THE EVALUATION PROCESS

What, then, is entailed in the evaluation process? As Figure 17.1 indicates, in order to regulate and control our marketing plan effectively, we need to use information which has been disaggregated to the degree that will enable us to locate precisely the causes of underperformance, and also to notice those areas of the company which are working well and which the marketing plan is therefore getting right.

The evaluation process locates the causes of underperformance while highlighting areas that are working successfully.

Three main types of measure are employed: 'market share analysis', 'marketing expenses to sales ratios' and 'customer tracking'.

Market share analysis

This measure is the one most frequently used by modern portfolio techniques of planning, and both short- and long-term objectives are set in these terms. The measure allows the company to evaluate how well it is doing in relation to the total market and to its competitors. Market shares may be calculated by value, by volume or by looking at specific types of market, such as replacement rather than original items – for instance, new cars only within the total car market. Other kinds of market share representation are also possible, depending on the point to be illustrated.

Marketing expenses to sales ratios

This ratio combines the amount spent on marketing activities with the sales which have been achieved by the company. These are important, but they are only broad measures which must be carefully interpreted. Detailed checks on marketing expenditure must, of course, always be maintained as part of good 'house keeping'.

Customer tracking

This monitors how customers view the company's products and its marketing activities, and includes a wide range of qualitative and quantitative measures of customer reactions from panel data, internal records of customer complaints, salesforce reports, focus group interviews and surveys.

THE AUDIT OF MARKETING OBJECTIVES, POLICIES AND ACTIVITIES

From time to time the company should conduct a complete review of marketing objectives, policies and activities on a company wide basis. Such a review is, perhaps, the most comprehensive approach to evaluating marketing effectiveness. This aims to examine and evaluate the success or otherwise of the marketing objectives and policies which have been guiding the company. This is a comprehensive review of both the activities of the company in relation to marketing, and of the environmental factors which are likely to bear upon their success or failure in achieving the objectives of the marketing plan. This is a very extensive and wide-ranging process, and is likely to occur less frequently than the more modest survey approach which is used to measure 'marketing effectiveness', setting itself a much more modest aim.

A comprehensive review of the company's marketing activities will reveal the success or failure of its marketing policies.

Summary

In this chapter we have looked at the nature, purpose and approaches to evaluating and controlling marketing activities and plans. Control is essential if the planning process is to be efficient and effective, although this area is often neglected, purposely or otherwise, by many marketing managers. A wide range of control mechanisms is available to the marketer, ranging from techniques such as efficiency control through to customer tracking. Finally, a complete and comprehensive review and evaluation of all marketing activities should take place from time to time.

Chapter 18
The Marketing Plan Budget

INTRODUCTION

In this final chapter we consider the importance and nature of determining and allocating budgets and resources to achieve the marketing plan. We shall look at the ways in which the marketing budget relates to the sales and marketing targets which were determined earlier in the marketing plan. The methods of arriving at the marketing budget and the relationship between sales forecasts and budgets will also be reviewed. Finally, we shall look at how budgets help in the control and evaluation process.

THE SIGNIFICANCE OF THE MARKETING BUDGET: RELATIONSHIP TO THE MARKETING PLAN

The aim of the marketing plan is, of course, to make profits, but in order to do so, it will be necessary to commit and dispense resources of various kinds, including financial resources. Marketing plans will set targets in a number of different areas – for example, for the portfolio of products or services involved, specific sales targets, in terms of volume or market share, will be set for individual products, including a specification of the time frame within which these targets are to be achieved. Targets will be set for each product, each sales division, down to each salesperson – every element will be expected to achieve a 'sales quota'.

In order to achieve these sales targets, resources – manpower, promotional activity, advertising, and so on – must be deployed, and an early decision relates to the amount which it is sensible to dedicate to the achievement of these objectives. Once a 'global figure' has been arrived at, based on a range of calculations which relate to the state of the company, its markets, competitor activity, other strategic objectives and competition from other centres of activity within the company – the amount will then be divided between the following:

❑ Salaries and staff costs.
❑ *Above the line*' costs – for example, commissioned promotional activity and advertising.
❑ *Below the line* expenditure – for example, sales promotions, price-reduction support costs, PR, and so on.

Targets set by top managers within the overall strategy of the company will often take account of sales price decisions, but a certain degree of discretion will typically be left up to the team devising and implementing the marketing plan, since the achievement of overall aims may require a certain amount of flexibility in order to take into account, for example, unforeseen problems or resistance in a particular area, or to take advantage of the extra possibilities offered by better-than-expected performance. An example here would concern the determination of beer prices in public houses. Brewing companies may price differentially, according to the area, and place their houses into certain 'bands', but they have always allowed their managers a certain amount of leeway in the prices which they finally set in order to accommodate and use the managers' knowledge of the characteristics of customers in a particular location.

Often, marketing expenditure will be organised systematically around the particular needs of particular products within the company's portfolio. Products which perform particularly well or particularly poorly will obviously require different levels of activity and, consequently, differential allocation of budgetary resources.

Marketing plan decisions, then, are the key determinants of the budget size and how it is to be allocated. The main aspects of the marketing plan which affect the budget are:

❑ Sales targets.
❑ Total marketing expenditure.
❑ Marketing mix decisions.
❑ Allocation of resources within the portfolio of products/services.

METHODS OF BUDGETING

The marketing budget is typically arrived at by one of three methods:

1. *Top-down planning* involves the upper echelons of the company in making decisions and simply passing them down to the rest of the company.
2. *Bottom-up planning* involves employees in planning and setting their own goals which are passed upwards to the top executives for approval.
3. *Goals down – plans up* is obviously a compromise between the first two styles. Overall goals are set by those at the top, but employees are crucial to the development of plans by means of which these objectives can be met.

This last method of budget setting is particularly effective in the setting of sales budgets, since those 'at the face' are likely to have a far better and more realistic notion of what sales revenues can be achieved and what kinds of resources may need to be deployed in order to achieve these targets. The factors which may influence the achievement of targets in these areas are notoriously complex and difficult to estimate, and it is very important to take advantage of the specialist knowledge which employees working in this area will have garnered over time. Marketing plan budgets, consequently, cannot be set in the way that other types of budgets can be, by simply applying a recipe or formula in a relatively mechanical way. The environment is constantly changing and the results or consequences of particular strategies are likely to be very difficult to predict accurately.

The importance of the marketing planning budget cannot be underestimated, but the market is constantly changing, making accurate prediction of strategies difficult.

Nevertheless, a marketing planning budget is extremely important. It brings the activities within the marketing area under the ambit of the overall corporate strategy which is being operated by an enterprise, and takes account of the overall budget which is being operated, and the way in which this relates to all the other activities which are taking place within the enterprise.

Often, the costs involved in the marketing plan are a very significant part of the overall operating costs of the company's operation. In this case, it is only sensible to attempt to plan these costs systematically, to attempt to forecast their effect, and to keep as close a control as possible over the way in which they are used.

Markets are, however, extremely uncertain. It is vital to have the best possible information on which to base plans and predictions. In some cases, of course, budgets are used for control. As we saw in the previous chapter, more budgetary control will be needed if budget estimates are uncertain.

FORECASTS AND CAPACITY - THE PROBLEM OF MATCHING

Setting budgets is confronted by the problem of matching the forecast demand from targeted consumers, with the capacity of the enterprise to produce the goods or to provide the services involved. This problem is especially thorny for three reasons:

1. Forecasting demand accurately is notoriously difficult.
2. Since there are always abiding uncertainties surrounding the factors which affect the production of goods or the provision of services – including operating conditions, performance, staff availability, and so on – it is often difficult to produce accurate estimates of available capacity too.
3. Factors such as seasonality or shifts in public taste may well affect the balance between demand and supply/capacity.

Matching supply and demand requires particular kinds of management actions. For example, demand can be dampened down by raising prices, if it exceeds the available supply, or excess capacity can be disposed of by price cutting, special offers or by increasing the budget allocation for advertising and promotion. Capacity to produce goods or the resources to provide a service can be sold off, thereby matching the supply and demand more closely, whereas under-capacity may be countered in the short term by subcontracting work to other organisations, or actively extending the premises, plant or manpower devoted to this area, including paying more for increased productivity from staff or providing extra working hours in the form of overtime.

ALLOCATING BUDGETS TO ELEMENTS OF THE MARKETING MIX: PROBLEMS AND ISSUES

Having determined the overall budget for marketing, it must be allocated to the various elements of the marketing mix – that is, to various marketing activities. We mentioned earlier the problem of matching expenditure on marketing activity with the profit/sales which such activity generates. We can explore this problem further by looking at the issues which arise when, for example, the promotional budget is set. Many of the problems which are outlined below for the promotional budget also apply when budget allocations to the other areas of the marketing mix are determined. When promotional budgets are set, the theory of 'diminishing returns' is generally used – extra spending on promotion should generate equal amounts of increased profit. Further expenditure is justified only to the point when the marginal return effectively ceases to exist.

This sounds like a fine principle, but the reality is that the marginal return from promotional (and other marketing) activities is notoriously difficult to measure. To begin with, promotional activity covers a wide range, including advertising (which we can measure as an item of expenditure), but also a plethora of above- and below-the-line activities, not to mention different sorts of publicity, good and bad, all of which contributes, in one way or another, to the performance of the products and to the firm itself. In addition, promotional activity has complex effects; some last a long time, others are very fleeting. How can we accommodate the long-term effects of promotional activity – for example, the accumulated goodwill of customers or the traditional reputation of a firm and its products?

In addition, it appears that there are certain rigidities in the way in which promotional spending is determined. Where the promotional budget is set according to the volume of sales (as a percentage of revenue), then what is spent follows, rather than determines, sales levels.

In fact, because of the imprecision involved and the severe problems involved in measuring effects or attributing causality, promotional (and other marketing activity) budgets tend to be set using rule-of-thumb methods, or as a response to competitor activity. Nevertheless, this is an area in which there is a growing sophistication and, thanks to the burgeoning use of powerful computing facilities, the possibility of using ever more sophisticated methods is now opening up for the non-specialist and the small enterprise. Promotional (and other marketing activity) budgets will increasingly be set using good practice such as:

Measuring the effects of promotional activity is extremely difficult, but the advantages of computerisation have made available more accurate information.

❑ *Empirical testing*; which, in the case of promotional budgets, for example, would entail relying on responses to mail-shots or by observing customer responses to promotional activities, such as in-store displays, special offers or advertising hoardings.

❑ *Mathematical modelling* is also increasingly being used in the budget-setting process. In the case of the promotional budget, therefore, this might involve, for example, bringing together consumer data with media characteristics, desired market share and records of past results. Regression analysis based on this data will indicate the likely cost of advertising and suggest the mixes of promotional activities which are likely to achieve these aims.

Budgetary considerations alone do not reflect a company's success or failure: the quality of marketing objectives also need to be evaluated.

BUDGETING AND THE EVALUATION AND CONTROL PROCESS

One of the main functions of the budget, of course, is to help in the evaluation and control process which was outlined in the preceding chapter. The budget will provide checks for the evaluation of the marketing plan, but it will also enable us to allocate the costs involved in the selling process. These include direct costs, which can be allocated to different brands, outlets, or salesperson in a relatively uncontroversial manner, but also indirect costs, such as administration, which can be attributed to every part of the organisation and tends to be allocated in an arbitrary manner according to criteria such as sales value. This represents another limitation of the use of budgetary data in order to evaluate effectiveness or profitability. It is often difficult to gauge the true significance of a particular product or the provision of a service in what seems like unprofitable conditions. Eliminating such items from the company portfolio because of their apparent unprofitability may reveal another function, such as maintaining appropriate productive capacity which would otherwise be unavailable in times of high demand, or serving as a means to dispose of extra capacity. Such charges also tend towards a progressive shift in the profitability of other brands, since fixed costs of production have to be borne by smaller numbers of remaining products, making them, in terms of these simplistic criteria, apparently less profitable. The allocation of fixed selling costs to products may make a product seem less profitable, but it is important to remember that the product may well still be making a contribution to the fixed costs, so that when it disappears, the fixed costs which have to be borne by the remaining products are increased by more than just the proportion which was allocated to the product.

The marketing budget is one of the main ways in which the profitability and performance of particular aspects of marketing activity are evaluated, as we have indicated. Although there are problems in using such measures in unsophisticated ways, there are, nevertheless, a large number of 'performance ratios' which are employed for a variety of reasons. For example, they may be used to measure the effectiveness of different aspects of marketing performance, such as the distribution system, the efficiency of individual employees or the value of a particular promotion. Sometimes cost and/or revenue data is combined with a wide range of diverse measures, such as:

❏ Value added per employee.
❏ Wages per employee.
❏ Sales per cubic metre of shelf space/per square metre of floor space.
❏ Sales per salesperson.
❏ Contribution per cubic metre of shelf space, per square metre of floor space or per employee.

❑ Net profit per cubic metre of shelf space, per square metre of floor space or per employee.
❑ Occupancy costs per square metre.
❑ Cost per salesperson call.

It is possible to extend this list exponentially. Every business has its own unique environmental characteristics, philosophy of management, culture, objectives and methods of working, so that we can imagine new measures and new ways of using the budget, with no real effort.

THE LIMITS OF BUDGETING AND FORECASTING

Everyone would agree that the pursuit of profit is the main objective for businessmen, and this tends to lead to a very single-minded focus on the budgeting process and the data it provides. Often, this focus tends to lose sight of the fact that it is the quality of marketing objectives which have to be related to the particular features of the enterprise and the markets within which it is operating, rather than the simplistic and highly general measures of accounting which lead to success.

Managers currently complain of the following when they rely on budgetary and forecasting procedures as the basis for marketing planning:

❑ Opportunities for profit are lost.
❑ Numbers in long-range plans appear meaningless.
❑ Objectives seem unrealistic.
❑ There is a lack of actionable marketing information.
❑ Interfunctional strife is generated.
❑ Managers become frustrated.
❑ There is a proliferation of products and markets.
❑ Promotional expenditure is wasted.
❑ Pricing becomes confused.
❑ There is growing vulnerability to environmental changes.
❑ There is a feeling of loss of control.

Financial measures in themselves are poor indicators of what a

Budgetary considerations alone do not reflect a company's success or failure: the quality of marketing objectives also need to be evaluated.

company is doing wrong or what it is doing right. Much more sophisticated measures are needed to estimate what marketing is trying to accomplish, rather than simply indirect reflections of a complex phenomena which is interacting in a dynamic commercial environment. Structured approaches should reflect two major considerations. First, we should try to ensure that when strengths and weaknesses of marketing plans are evaluated, measures are sensitive and wide-ranging, rather than simply budgetary elements. Secondly, we should try to ensure that this kind of analysis is presented within a logical and rigorous framework.

Summary

In this chapter we have looked at the budgeting process with respect to the marketing plan. We have examined how this process relates to the marketing plan itself and some of the approaches to setting the overall budget, and the problems and issues in allocating this effectively to different areas of marketing activity. We have also discussed how the budget relates to the evaluation and control of marketing performance, and looked at some of the pitfalls of a narrow view of what constitutes effective marketing performance.

Index